Tucholsky  Wagner  Zola  Scott  Sydow  Freud  Schlegel
Turgenev  Wallace  Fonatne
Twain  Walther von der Vogelweide  Fouqué  Friedrich II. von Preußen
Weber  Freiligrath  Frey
Kant  Ernst
Fechner  Fichte  Weiße Rose  von Fallersleben  Richthofen  Frommel
Hölderlin
Engels  Fielding  Eichendorff  Tacitus  Dumas
Fehrs  Faber  Flaubert
Eliasberg  Ebner Eschenbach
Feuerbach  Maximilian I. von Habsburg  Fock  Zweig  Eliot
Ewald  Vergil
Goethe  London
Elisabeth von Österreich
Mendelssohn  Balzac  Shakespeare  Dostojewski  Ganghofer
Trackl  Lichtenberg  Rathenau  Doyle  Gjellerup
Stevenson  Hambruch
Mommsen  Tolstoi  Lenz  Hanrieder  Droste-Hülshoff
Thoma
Dach  von Arnim  Hägele  Hauff  Humboldt
Verne  Hagen  Hauptmann
Karrillon  Reuter  Rousseau  Gautier
Garschin
Defoe  Baudelaire
Damaschke  Hebbel
Descartes
Hegel  Kussmaul  Herder
Wolfram von Eschenbach  Schopenhauer
Dickens  Rilke  George
Bronner  Darwin  Melville  Grimm  Jerome
Campe  Horváth  Aristoteles  Bebel  Proust
Bismarck  Vigny  Barlach  Voltaire  Federer  Herodot
Gengenbach  Heine
Storm  Casanova  Tersteegen  Grillparzer  Georgy
Chamberlain  Lessing  Langbein  Gilm  Gryphius
Brentano  Lafontaine
Strachwitz  Claudius  Schiller  Kralik  Iffland  Sokrates
Bellamy  Schilling
Katharina II. von Rußland  Gerstäcker  Raabe  Gibbon  Tschechow
Löns  Hesse  Hoffmann  Gogol  Wilde  Gleim  Vulpius
Luther  Heym  Hofmannsthal  Morgenstern
Roth  Klee  Hölty  Goedicke
Heyse  Klopstock  Kleist
Luxemburg  Puschkin  Homer  Mörike
Horaz  Musil
Machiavelli  La Roche
Navarra  Aurel  Musset  Kierkegaard  Kraft  Kraus
Lamprecht  Kind  Moltke
Nestroy  Marie de France  Kirchhoff  Hugo
Laotse  Ipsen  Liebknecht
Nietzsche  Nansen  Ringelnatz
Marx
von Ossietzky  Lassalle  Gorki  Klett  Leibniz
May  vom Stein  Lawrence  Irving
Petalozzi  Knigge
Platon  Michelangelo  Kafka
Pückler  Kock
Sachs  Poe  Liebermann
de Sade  Praetorius  Mistral  Zetkin  Korolenko

The publishing house tredition has created the series **TREDITION CLASSICS**. It contains classical literature works from over two thousand years. Most of these titles have been out of print and off the bookstore shelves for decades.

The book series is intended to preserve the cultural legacy and to promote the timeless works of classical literature. As a reader of a **TREDITION CLASSICS** book, the reader supports the mission to save many of the amazing works of world literature from oblivion.

The symbol of **TREDITION CLASSICS** is Johannes Gutenberg (1400 – 1468), the inventor of movable type printing.

With the series, tredition intends to make thousands of international literature classics available in printed format again – worldwide.

All books are available at book retailers worldwide in paperback and in hardcover. For more information please visit: www.tredition.com

tredition was established in 2006 by Sandra Latusseck and Soenke Schulz. Based in Hamburg, Germany, tredition offers publishing solutions to authors and publishing houses, combined with worldwide distribution of printed and digital book content. tredition is uniquely positioned to enable authors and publishing houses to create books on their own terms and without conventional manufacturing risks.

For more information please visit: www.tredition.com

# A Letter from Major Robert Carmichael-Smyth to His Friend, the Author of 'The Clockmaker'

Robert Carmichael-Smyth

# Imprint

This book is part of the TREDITION CLASSICS series.

Author: Robert Carmichael-Smyth
Cover design: toepferschumann, Berlin (Germany)

Publisher: tredition GmbH, Hamburg (Germany)
ISBN: 978-3-8491-4827-0

www.tredition.com
www.tredition.de

Copyright:
The content of this book is sourced from the public domain.

The intention of the TREDITION CLASSICS series is to make world literature in the public domain available in printed format. Literary enthusiasts and organizations worldwide have scanned and digitally edited the original texts. tredition has subsequently formatted and redesigned the content into a modern reading layout. Therefore, we cannot guarantee the exact reproduction of the original format of a particular historic edition. Please also note that no modifications have been made to the spelling, therefore it may differ from the orthography used today.

# PREFACE.

"It is the duty—the imperative duty—of every individual (however humble) to express conscientiously, but calmly, his public opinions, for by such means truth is elicited." [1] Hence it may be permitted the writer of the annexed Letter to observe, that a momentous question is now brought to the notice of the people of Great Britain,—that it ought not to be neglected, until perhaps a voice from her colonial children may go forth proclaiming "it is too late,"[see Note 64]—for then the opportunity of uniting in firm and friendly bonds of union "this wondrous empire on which the solar orb never sets" will have passed away for ever.

— —"Dum loquimur fugerit invida Ætas: carpe diem quàm minimùm credula postero."

[1] Montgomery Martin's History of the British Colonies, 1843; and to that work the writer of the following pages begs to refer all those who take an interest in the British North American Colonies. And if so humble an individual might be allowed to offer his advice, he would strongly recommend the republication, in a volume by itself, of the part connected with the North American Colonies.

# INTRODUCTION.

"I shall tell you
A pretty tale; it may be, you have heard it;
But, since it serves my purpose, I will venture
To scale't again."

"The duty of Government is first to regulate the stream of Emigration, so that if a man be determined on leaving the United Kingdom he may settle in one of its Colonies." — *Montgomery Martin, 1843.*

"At this moment, when renewed attention is turned to all the Routes which, during ages past, have from time to time been talked about, as best fitted for a link of communication between the Atlantic and Pacific Oceans," — we call upon the people of Great Britain and her Government to reflect, that — the best and shortest link of communication — the great link required to unite all her dominions in one powerful chain — is now in her own possession, — that — "it *is* in vain to inculcate feelings of brotherhood among mankind by moral influence alone; a sense of community of interest *must* be also established," — that Great Britain can, in the opening of the Route proposed, at the same time employ her own Children at home and abroad, as well as her own continually increasing Capital.

That — "we have superabundance of Capital — a plethora of Talent — Scientific and Commercial — they only want an outlet to be beneficially employed." — *Morning Herald, 7th February, 1849.*

That — "the Expansion of Capital would soon reach its ultimate boundary, if that boundary itself did not continually increase."

That — "what the Legislature should desire and promote is not a greater saving, but a greater return to savings, either by improved cultivation, or by access to more fertile lands in other quarters of the globe."

That — "the Railway operations of the various nations of the world may be looked upon as a sort of competition for the overflowing Capital of the countries where Profits are low and Capital abundant." — *J. S. Mill, Polit. Econ.*

That—"each nation derives greater benefit from having an increasing market in one of its own provinces, than in a foreign country."

That—"the possession of remote territories, is the only thing which can secure to the population of a country those advantages derived from an easy outlet, or prospect of outlet, to those persons who may be ill provided for at home." —*Lord Brougham.*

That—"we have an immense Colonial Empire. To its resources and exigencies we now seem for the first time to awaken.[see Note 46] Hitherto we have been content to consider it as a magnificent incumbrance, that testified to our greatness but had nothing to do with our interests or the welfare of our population." —*The Times, 20th January, 1849.*

And that—"it must be acknowledged as a principle, that the Colonies of England are an integral part of this country." —*D'Israeli.*

Again—"In certain parts of the Empire transportation was a very valuable punishment, but there ought to be natural limits to it. Transportation was very well in the infancy of a Colony, but as it became more peopled and civilized, it was undesirable to deluge it with a convict population. The subject of abolishing the penalty of transportation was one of very great importance." —*Lord Brougham, 1849.*

"But what mean I
To speak so true at first? My office is
To noise abroad....
I have the letter here; yes, here it is:"

[Pg 1]

"The time has come when the great American and Colonial route of travelling must commence at Halifax." [2] —*Great Western Letter Bag.* Yes! and be carried on to Frazer's River. [3]

[2] Nova Scotia.

[3] New Caledonia.

TO
MY WORTHY AND MUCH ESTEEMED FRIEND,
THE AUTHOR OF "THE CLOCKMAKER."

My Dear Friend,

Often have I looked back to the pleasant hours we passed on board the good brig Tyrian, when, in the spring of 1838, we were quietly floating over the waves of the broad Atlantic.[see Note 1] Never do I remember to have crossed them so smoothly, and never certainly with more agreeable companions. One of our party has long since departed for that country from whose bourn no traveller returns. Poor Fairbanks! you knew him well and valued his friendship—knew him to be a kind and a good man, and that he loved his country well. Had he been as anxious to introduce Railways into it as he was zealous about his Shubenacadie Canal, he might perhaps have served it more effectually.[see Notes 2 and 37] Another of our party, a true and hearty lover of his country, is still amongst you; may his powerful mind so direct his great abilities as to enable him to use them for his country's good; for much may yet be done for Nova Scotia. Both he and you, I know well, have a friendly feeling towards me, and you may perhaps have sometimes regretted, though not so warmly as I have done (living as you both have [Pg 2] been for years in the midst of political excitement), that we have been so completely separated. With this short preface, as an excuse for introducing your names, I will now proceed, by recalling that moment so full of excitement at the time and never to be forgotten,—when, to our astonishment, we first saw the great ship Syrius steaming down directly in the wake of the Tyrian. She was the first steamer, I believe, that ever crossed the Atlantic for New York, and was then on her way back to England. You will, I dare say, recollect the prompt decision of Commander Jennings to carry his mail bags on board the steamer, and our equally prompt decision not to quit our sailing craft, commanded as she was by so kind and so excellent an officer. You will, I dare say, recollect how soon flew the question through the captain's trumpet, "Will you take charge of the mail?" "Yes, but be quick;" and the trembling anxiety with which we watched mail bag after mail bag hoisted up the deep waist of the Tyrian; then lowered into the small boat below,—tossed about between the vessels, and finally all safely placed on board the Syrius. It was a bold measure; for had one mail bag been lost, our gallant commander would in all probability have been severely censured, if

it had not cost him his commission: as it was, I believe, he received
the thanks of the Admiralty. You will also, no doubt, remember
well the lively discussion the sight of this great steam ship caused
amongst us, and how earnestly I expressed my wish, that the people
of Halifax should bestir themselves, and not allow, without a strug-
gle, British mails and British passengers thus to be taken past their
very doors.[see Note 3] And now that we have lived to see established what we then discussed (and about which the pen of the
Clockmaker's companion was not idle),[see Note 4] the great steam
ship road from and to Liverpool and Halifax, you will not perhaps
be astonished that (like the fly on the wheel) so humble an individual as your old fellow passenger should [Pg 3] have fancied when
steaming (as he has since often done) over the waves of that same
Atlantic, that he too[see Note 5] had had something to say in creating all the smoke he saw rising before him. Of one thing, however,
he is certain—that his companions, Fairbanks, Howe and Haliburton (no insignificant names), had determined, before leaving the
Tyrian, that as soon as they reached London they would wait upon
the Colonial minister—point out to him the necessity and importance of a steam communication from the mother country to her
children in the west, and plead the cause of Halifax;[see Note 6]
and, if I am not mistaken, Fairbanks and Howe proceeded first to
Liverpool to make some inquiries about expense, &c. &c. Be this
however as it may, it is all now matter of no consequence—the great
nautical high road between England and her North American Colonies has long been established beyond a question, and the enterprising Cunard has shown by his splendid steam vessels, that it may be
depended upon beyond a doubt, as a regular, a safe and an easy
communication.[see Note 38] To him, therefore, are due the thanks
of the public, and the credit of accomplishing this much wished-for
route.

> "Whilst others bravely thought, he
> nobly dar'd."

But, my dear friend, in an age like the present, shall such a victory
content us? most assuredly not! The time has come when our great
Colonial land route of travelling must reach from Halifax to Frazer's
River, from the Atlantic to the Pacific—and there is still a grand and
a noble undertaking that must yet be accomplished—must be per-

formed by Great Britain and her colonies—an undertaking that will open a mine of wealth to all concerned[see Note 7] (not the wealth of gold, but of commerce and trade). But to proceed—and here again I must tax your memory. [Pg 4] You will, no doubt, recollect, that after the King of Holland had given his decision in the year 1831 as to our disputed boundary with America, which had been referred to him, and that all eyes were fixed upon that question,[see Note 65] which had become very serious and difficult to settle, his Grace the Duke of Wellington, in speaking on the subject,[see Note 8] alluded to another very important boundary question (then little thought of by the public),[see Note 9] and his Grace pointed to the Oregon.[see Note 33] The discussions and difficulties that afterwards arose before the final disposal of that dispute, most assuredly marked its importance, and proved that the ever-watchful talent of the Duke had not been attracted to that spot, without cause.

> "We thank the gods
> Our Rome has such a soldier!"

Montgomery Martin says, "But for the Hudson's Bay Company, England would probably have been shut out from the Pacific." Be that as it may, we had at all events, one statesman's watchful eye upon that ocean, and the very important question is now disposed of for ever, leaving open to England another most valuable high road, with the making of which we (again like the fly on the wheel) think we must have something to do; at all events, we may discuss and talk about it,—as in the Tyrian we formerly did about the great Steam Line from and to Liverpool and Halifax. But to proceed seriously. Did his Grace, let it be asked, when pointing to our North-Western boundary line, look forward at that time to the shores of the Pacific as being "the end of the West and the beginning of the East?" Did his Grace's imagination picture to his mind's eye swarms of human beings from Halifax, from New Brunswick, from Quebec, from Montreal, from Byetown, from Kingston, from [Pg 5] Toronto, from Hamilton, the Red River Settlement, &c. &c. &c., rushing across the rocky mountains of Oregon with the produce of the West in exchange for the riches of the East? Did his Grace imagine the Pacific Ocean alive with all descriptions of vessels sailing and steaming from our magnificent Colonies—New Zealand, Van Diemen's Land, New South Wales, New Holland, from Borneo and the West Coast of China, from the Sandwich Islands, and a thousand other places, all carrying the rich productions of the East, and landing them at the commencement of the West, — to be forwarded and distributed throughout our North American provinces, and to be delivered in Thirty Days at the ports of Great Britain? Did his Grace foresee that steam would bring Halifax within ten days of Liverpool? That a Railway would make Halifax only ten or fifteen days distant from the north-west coast of North America, (and that the Sandwich Islands would not be ten days further off?) whence steamers might be despatched with the mails from England for Pekin, Canton, Australia, New Zealand, &c. &c. &c.; and did his Grace look forward to the rolling masses of treasure that would be sure to travel on such a girdle line of communication as that? Did his Grace then weigh and consider that "to the inventive genius of her sons England owes the foundation of her commercial greatness. We will not go the length of asserting that she retains her proud pre-eminence solely upon the condition of keeping twenty years ahead of other nations in the practice of mechanical arts. But there is no question, that *a fearful proportion of our fellow subjects hold their prosperity upon no other tenure*, and quite independently of what may be done by our rivals it is of vast importance to our increasing population that the conquest over nature should proceed unchecked?" [*Quarterly Review, December, 1848.*] And did his Grace look forward and foresee that between the [Pg 6] north-eastern and north-western shores of America, and through our loyal, long-tried and devoted North American colonies,[see Note 10] there might be undertaken a great, a noble, and a most important work, that would give remunerative employment to the population, to the wealth, and to the inventive genius of England? Did his Grace, in short, look forward to a *grand National Railway from the Atlantic to the Pacific*?[see Note 60] If not, let his Grace do so now! Let the people of Great Britain do so! — let her colonial minister. Startling as it may at first appear, a little reflection will show that England and her children have the power to make it; that it must be done; and will become valuable property — for it would increase our commerce and trade to an extent not easy to calculate.[see Note 11] But such a noble work must not be looked upon merely as a money question, — although if only considered in that light, — England must reflect that if she wishes and intends to retain her high pre-eminence amongst the nations of the earth, she must most assuredly pay for it. No country can have all the blessings and advantages of England and have them for nothing, nor can she retain them without great exertion. Her accumulated wealth cannot be allowed to remain idle—nor will it.[see Note 12] No one will deny for a moment that every economy that will make the poor man richer and happier ought to be practised;[see Note 39] but let us take care that we do not, from too strong a desire to retain that wealth which Providence has thrown into the lap of England[see Note 13] even in the midst of war, [see Note 14] deprive her labouring children of legitimate employment and just remuneration, (all that the industrious classes of our fellow-countrymen require.) But the undertaking proposed has even a higher claim to our attention. *It is the great link required to unite in one powerful chain the whole English race.* [Pg 7] Let then our Railway Kings, and our Iron Kings, our princely merchants, and our lords millionnaires—let the stirring and active spirits of the age—the great reformers and the modern politicians, many of whom are now proclaiming through the land that economy alone can save the country—[see Note 15]condescend for a short time even, to consider the undertaking here proposed; and say, if they can, that (even should it be executed at an immense expense) it would not produce a great and beneficial forward movement, and be a present happy employment, and a future perpetual source of wealth to England and her children. Let them consider also that "the social advancement which the modern improvement of Railways is calculated to effect has added a new faculty to man in the facilities which it affords of communication between province and province, and between nation and nation. Nor does it seem too much to say, that it will be the means of binding all the nations of the earth into one family, with mutual interests, and with the mutual desire of promoting the prosperity of their neighbours, in order that they may enhance their own, and forming thereby the most powerful antagonistic principle to war that the earth has ever known." [*Bradshaw's Almanack, 1849.*] Again, what says the Quarterly: "We trust our readers of all politics will cordially join with us in a desire, not inappropriate at the commencement of a new year, that the wonderful discovery which it has pleased the Almighty to impart to us, instead of becoming amongst us a subject of angry dispute, may in every region of the globe bring the human family into friendly communication; that it may dispel national prejudices; assuage animosities—in short, that, by creating a feeling of universal gratitude to the powers from which it has proceeded, it may produce on earth peace and good-will [Pg 8] towards men." And where, let it be asked, can this wonderful discovery, this great power of steam,[see Note 16] be called into action so effectually and so usefully, not only for Great Britain, but for mankind in general, than in that parallel of latitude[see Note 17] in which (*all barrier difficulties and all cause for war being now removed*) would naturally flow in full tide the civilization, arts and sciences that invariably follow in the wake of Englishmen? Then as to the difficulties of the undertaking, let us recollect that an eminent engineer, previous to the construction of the Liverpool and Manchester Line, said, "No man in his senses would attempt a Railroad over Chat Moss:" his calculation was that it would cost £270,000. Yet the genius of George Stephenson afterwards surmounted the difficulty at a cost of £40,000, though the work was commenced when engineering science was less understood than now. Let us also listen to the Quarterly, "Steam as applied to locomotion by sea and land is the great wonder-worker of the age. For many years we have been so startled by such a succession of apparent miracles, we have so often seen results which surpassed and falsified all the deductions of sober calculations, and so brief an interval has elapsed between the day when certain performances were classed by men of science as among impossibilities, and that wherein those same performances had almost ceased to be remarkable from their frequency, that we might almost be excused if we regarded the cloud-compelling demon, with somewhat of the reverence which the savage pays to his superior, when he worships as omnipotent any power whose limits he cannot himself perceive." With such a power[see Note 18] (so eloquently described) at our command, and such magnificent results to be obtained from it, shall England hesitate? shall the expenditure of a few millions [Pg 9] check such a noble work? shall the Rocky Mountains be a barrier? mountains never yet properly explored, and of which almost all we know is that (as my friend Colonel Bloomfield observed) we nearly went to war to be allowed to cross them. And what are the expenses of war? Between the years 1797 and 1815, 630 millions of money were expended for carrying on war. Again, the very magnitude of the undertaking and length of the Railway is in its favour, for—

listen again to the Quarterly: "We believe it may be affirmed without fear of contradiction, that the working details of a Railway are invariably well executed in proportion to their magnitude. A little Railway—like a little war—is murderous to those engaged and ruinous to those who pay for it." Now if in England experience has taught all this,—shall the good people of Halifax, New Brunswick, Quebec, Montreal, Toronto, &c., be allowed, perhaps encouraged, to go on slowly endeavouring (at an immense expense and outlay for such young communities) to make a variety of small Railways,[see Note 40] thus acknowledged to be ruinous, and the mother country remain quietly looking on when she has now the power of greatly assisting them, and to her own advantage, by planning and arranging one grand route and system of Lines throughout the whole country,[see Note 19] and under Providence the means of opening that route in an incredible short space of time? Let then England, her North American colonies, and the Hudson's Bay Company, join heart and hand, and with the great power of steam which it has pleased the Almighty to place at the command of man, there will soon arise a work that will be the wonder and admiration of the age—and such a mercantile and colonizing road will be open to Great Britain, that at no future period, (at least within the imagination of man,) will she ever again have to complain of too great a population on her soil, and too small a market for her labour.

[Pg 10] Let us now then proceed, my dear friend, to consider how this great work might be commenced, and its probable results when accomplished. In the first place let us look a little to the immense annual cost to England for her prisons and her convicts,[see Notes 47 and 50]—much of that crime arising probably from the want of employment, and consequent poverty.[see Note 20] Even at this moment five millions are spoken of as a sum required to be expended in new prisons for a favourite system.[see Note 41] In 1836 it was suggested "as well worthy of consideration, whether it would not be advisable to cease transporting convicts at so great a cost to distant settlements, and instead to send them to a nearer place of exile, where their labour might be rendered in so great a degree valuable, as speedily to return to the Mother Country the whole of the charge incurred for their conveyance" [*The Progress of the Nation, by A. R. Porter, Esq.*];[see Note 21] and where could England better employ her convict labour, than on a work that would be of such vast and lasting importance to herself, to her colonies, and to mankind in general? It was also observed, by the same author, "If gangs of convict labourers were placed a little beyond the verge of civilization, and employed in clearing and enclosing lands, constructing roads, building bridges, the land thus prepared and improved would meet with ready purchasers at prices which would well repay the Government their previous outlay." It may be objected by some, that the expense of the troops necessary to guard the convicts would be very great, and would be a heavy burden to this country. To them I must use the words of the "Times," when suggesting the grant of colonial lands to be annexed to the performance of military duties. "Subsidiary to and connected with this arrangement [Pg 11] might be devised another, by which soldiers of good character might be discharged after ten years service, and rewarded with small freeholds in the colonies. They might be bound to appear on duty at certain periods, and for a certain duration of time, as our pensioners are at present." And if soldiers of six or eight years service were sent out in charge of the convicts, that unpleasant duty would be of very short duration before they would meet with their reward. Added to which, it has been suggested by my friend Captain Wood, of the Hon. East India Company's service, that the Indians might be very usefully employed on this duty,[see Note 48] somewhat in the same manner as the natives in India are encouraged to look after European soldiers who desert their colours. In alluding to the pensioners of Great Britain, it is only due to Lieut.-Col. Tulloch to render our honest thanks to him, for the introduction through his indefatigable exertions of this most important feature in a new military system. Not only has he added to the respectability, comfort, and happiness of many a worn out old soldier, but he has also provided a very imposing force of veterans ready at any moment to support the laws of their country; and, should unfortunately such an occasion ever arise, of opposing all feeling of disloyalty to their beloved sovereign. [see Note 42] Lieut.-Col. Tulloch may well feel proud of the result of his labours. This system of pensions alluded to by the "Times" would become extremely applicable to the troops employed in guarding the convicts on the proposed Atlantic and Pacific Railway, and small villages, and ultimately cities, would, no doubt, arise from such a source: but even the first outlay caused by the employment of the convicts on such a work cannot be considered as any extra expense to government; for these convicts must be fed, must be employed, and must be guarded somewhere: and it will be shown hereafter that [Pg 12] government will be reimbursed not only her expenditure on account of the convicts, but also her expenditure on account of the troops required to guard them. In making his suggestions for the employment of the convicts in 1836, Mr. Porter says, "There is unhappily but too much reason for believing that the whole number of labourers who could be thus profitably employed might be furnished from the criminal population of Great Britain." And by a return given at the same time, it is shown that the number of convicts from 1825 to 1833, both years inclusive, was 22,138, and that return did not include all the penal settlements. The "Times" of the 18th January, 1848, in speaking of the expenditure of the country, says, "Convicts at home and abroad have mounted from £111,306 to £378,000; certainly the law of increase is strongly marked on the expense of crime." "If any body will cut down this figure, he will earn the gratitude of the nation." This last expression of the Times has more particular reference to the expense incurred for Ireland, but will no doubt be acknowledged to be equally true as bearing upon the enormous general increase of convict expenditure; and the more I reflect on this subject, the more do I feel convinced that the employment of convict labour in the Rocky Mountains,[see Note 22] and at several other points of the Line of this proposed great National work, would produce a most beneficial result, as a means of reducing the amount of crime, as even an immediate saving of transport expense to England (unless indeed all distant penal settlements are to be finally abandoned),[see Notes 21 and 45] and as an ultimate great advantage both to her own commerce, and to that of her colonies; and here let it be recollected, that there is a feeling abroad "to force upon government and the legislature a bold and manly course in dealing with crime in general:" that the [Pg 13] magnificent prisons now built are considered "unjust to the labouring poor, whose humble dwelling, with coarse and scanty food, is mocked by the grandeur and beauty of the prison, as well as by the idle and comfortable entertainment within its wall;" and it has been remarked by a public journal in a warning voice, "to make prisons palaces is the way to turn palaces into prisons."[see Note 34] But enough has been said on this subject at present, and we will now consider again the working out of this great undertaking. We will suppose, in the first place, active, intelligent, and scientific young men to be sent to the Rocky Mountains,[see Note 49] to ascertain the best spot at which to cross them, and the best port (if the mouth of Frazer's River will not answer), on the western shore of North America, within, of course, the Hudson's Bay Company's territory, for a great commercial harbour and railway terminus. Then let a grand line of Railway be marked out from Halifax to that spot, and let all local towns or districts that have sufficient capital and labour to undertake any part of that Line, have the benefit of the profits of the whole Line, in proportion to the parts they may finish. No convict labour need interfere with them. But in such districts as are at present so thinly inhabited as to have no working population, and no capital to expend, let the work be commenced by England, by her capital, and her convicts;[see Note 23] and let government encourage and facilitate the formation of a great Atlantic and Pacific Railway Company, by obtaining from parliament a national guarantee for the completion of the work;[see Note 51] first, of course, having entered into arrangements with the Hudson's Bay Company, and her North American provinces, for the security of such sums of money as may be advanced by way of loan from Great Britain.

[Pg 14] To Englishmen we would say then, in the words of the Rev. C. G. Nicolay, "We have at home a superabundant population,[see Note 24] subject to a very rapid increase on any reduction of the price, if but of the necessaries of life,—how can it be better employed than in seeking, with its own advance in social position, and means of acquiring its comforts, if not its luxuries, the spread of our free institutions—equal laws—and holy religion. We desire an enlarged sphere for commercial enterprise. New markets for our manufactures; these every fresh colony supplies in its measure. If then the Oregon be what it appears to be, if its climate, soil, agriculture, and commercial capabilities be as represented, why leave its future destiny to time and circumstances?" We would say to the Hudson's Bay Company in the words of Mr. James Edward Fitzgerald, "You have the power of becoming the founders of a New State, perhaps of a new empire, or of arresting for a time, for you cannot ultimately prevent, the march of mankind in their career of victory

20

over the desolate and uncultivated parts of the earth. For now nearly two centuries your sway has extended over half a continent, and
as yet you have left nothing behind you in all that vast country, to
bear witness to your power and your riches. Now a new destiny is
before you; you may, if you will, place your names beside those
who have devoted themselves to the noble task of stimulating and
directing the enterprising genius of their fellow countrymen, who
have prolonged the existence of their nation by giving a new life to
its offspring." And we would then call upon England, her North
American provinces, and the Hudson's Bay Company, to employ
their wealth and power to unite in one great unbroken iron chain,
the Mother Country with her distant Children, and, in spite of Nature's difficulties, carry steam across the Rocky Mountains.[see Note
25]

[Pg 15] From childhood I have been accustomed to look upon the
power of England as irresistible, — morally, physically,[see Note 35]
and intellectually, — she has now in this age the command of mind
and matter sufficient to enable her almost to move the earth, and
shall the tunnel under the Thames, the tube over the Conway, and
the bridge over the Menai, be our only wonders? How well do I
remember the delight with which I have listened to the anecdote
told of Mr. Pitt, who, when he was informed that it was impracticable to carry into effect some orders he had given about heavy ord-
nance being sent to Portsmouth within a certain time, "Not possible?" exclaimed Mr. Pitt, "then send them by the Mail."[see Note 26]
With the same feeling of pride and delight have I heard in later days
of the artillery officer's remark, when it was whispered to him by
another that it would not be possible to place their guns in some
wished for position; "My dear fellow," said the commanding officer, "I have the order in my pocket." Let England only commence
the Railway from Halifax to the Pacific, with the order to cross the
Rocky Mountains in the pocket of her sons, and the accomplishment
of the undertaking will soon reward the labour, courage and skill
which would undoubtedly be exhibited. Sir Alexander Mackenzie
inscribed in large characters, with vermillion, this brief memorial,
on the rocks of the Pacific, "Alexander Mackenzie from Canada by
land the 22nd of July, 1794." Who will be the first engineer to in-
scribe upon the Rocky Mountains "On this day engineer A. B. pi-

loted the first locomotive engine across the Rocky Mountains;" and what then will be the feeling of Englishmen, when even now Steam is considered the "exclusive offspring of British genius, fostered and sustained by British enterprise and British capital!" We have seen that on the highest habitable spot of the Mountains of the Alps stands a [Pg 16] monument of war, placed there by the hand of a powerful man in the pride of victory over his fellow-men, and in honour of his companion in arms. We trust before long that on the highest habitable spot of the Rocky Mountains will stand a monument of peace, placed there by an enterprising nation in honour of the victory of science over nature, and in memory of some enterprising son.

After all her wars, her victories and her revolutions, in what condition is France?

What may not England expect to be with all her victories over nature—her trade and commerce?[see Note 52] May she march forward in her career of peace as bravely, as nobly, and as proudly as she did in that of war; and may she now take as great an interest in, and make the same exertions for, the welfare and happiness not only of her own people, but of those of other nations in all quarters of the globe, as she did in former days for their protection from a desolating foe.

What the ultimate consequences of such a link of connection would be, are indeed far beyond the reach of the human mind to foresee; but its immediate results stand out apparently to the most common observer. In the first place, Cape Horn (*the roughest point to weather in the whole world*) would be avoided. In the next, the long passage by the Cape of Good Hope to innumerable places in the Pacific Ocean would become also unnecessary. In both these cases a great amount of time (which in commerce is money) would be saved. Again, it would be no longer necessary to send goods by the route of the Hudson's Bay[see Note 27] to the territories of that Company; and thus *a climate horrible in winter and summer*, would also be avoided.[see Note 44] Then one view of the map of the world will show that the proposed terminus of the Atlantic and Pacific Railway at Frazer's River, taken as a centre, would bring [Pg 17] New Zealand, New South Wales, in fact, Australia, New Guinea,

Borneo, Canton, Pekin, all within fifty days' sail of that point; and taking the Sandwich Islands as a centre point, (where there is a fine harbour, and where a depôt of coals might be established), which could be reached in ten days, all the before-named places would be brought within twenty days for steam navigation, other points, such as the Friendly Islands, &c., might be selected for further depôts of coals. Again, from the terminus of the proposed railway the mails from England could be despatched to all the before-mentioned places, and the formation of a great steam navigation company, with a grant from government in the same way as a grant was made to the Atlantic Steam Navigation Company to Halifax, would insure magnificent steamers for the conveyance of these mails, and would secure also to the Hudson's Bay Company an immense consumption of their coal. Last, though not least of all, this Railway route across the continent of North America would ensure to England at all times a free communication with her East India possessions. It is true that at present there is no difficulty in that respect, and the indefatigable exertions of Lieutenant Waghorn and of other enterprising people, amongst them my friend Major Head, have opened to the British public and to the East India Company a quick and speedy communication with India. But let the public reflect, and let the Government reflect, that, in the event of a European war, we might be called upon to defend and keep open that communication at an immense expenditure of life and money, and indeed it might even be closed against us; whereas the proposed Line across the continent of America would be within our own dominions, and would not oblige us to interfere or meddle with any continental wars to enjoy its free use. No time ought to be lost in the commencement of this national undertaking.

[Pg 18] If then Government took the initiative, it might obtain the consent of Parliament, and proceed to appoint a Board of General Arrangement and Control, consisting, say, of fifteen Commissioners: three on the part of Great Britain, three to be named by the Hudson's Bay Company, three to be appointed by the Government of Nova Scotia, three by that of New Brunswick, and three on the part of Canada; all these latter of course with the approval of their respective Governors. It may appear that the North American Provinces would thus have a greater proportion of Commissioners; but as each of these Colonies have Governments independent of each other, they may be considered as separate Companies, although we take them as one when considered as the North American Provinces. These fifteen gentlemen might be all Members of Parliament; thus the system of representatives from the Colonies, so often suggested and spoken of, could be commenced, and the Colonists thus made practically aware that they are *an integral part of this country.* These Commissioners could be authorized to make all the necessary arrangements for the security of the monies proposed to be advanced by the Government of Great Britain, and should be instructed to draw up the general Articles of Agreement between the high contracting parties; and Government might be authorized by Parliament to open an account with these Commissioners, who as a Body might be called "The Atlantic and Pacific Railway Board of Control," and under its auspices a public Company might be formed, refunding to the Government all previous outlay.

Our North American provinces are close at hand, and during the approaching summer all the necessary arrangements might be made for the reception of a great number of convicts in different locations; and, in the first instance, they might be sent to Halifax and Quebec,[see Note 53] where they [Pg 19] could be received immediately, not certainly in palaces, but in very good wood huts; at both these places they could also be at once set to work in unloading the vessels sent from England with the necessary stores for the commencement of this great national work, and in preparing and levelling the situations of the respective termini; for of course at both these stations great government as well as private wharfs would be established. Again: another portion could be sent at once from New South Wales to the port fixed upon on the north-west coast of North America, in the Hudson's Bay Company's territory:[see Note 67] there they could be put to work in the same way — to unload vessels bringing in stores, to cut down and prepare timber, level and get ready the site of the terminus. And it appears very necessary that preparation should be made for the reception of a large body at the Red River Settlement, that point being a very important spot in the Line proposed. Let us see what Montgomery Martin says about it.[see Note 28]

The Bishop of Montreal, in 1844, says, "The soil, which is alluvial, is beyond example rich and productive, and withal so easily worked, that, although it does not quite come up to the description of the Happy Islands—reddit ubi cererem tellus inarata quot annis—there is an instance, I was assured, of a farm in which the owner, with comparatively light labour in the preparatory processes, had taken a wheat crop out of the same land for eighteen successive years, never changing the crop, never manuring the land, and never suffering it to lie fallow, and that the crop was abundant to the last; and, with respect to the pasture and hay, they are to be had ad libitum, as nature gives them in the open plains." Again, speaking of import goods: "All these articles are brought across from Hudson's Bay, a distance of several hundred miles, in boats, and these boats are drawn across the portages [Pg 20] on rollers, or in some places carried upon waggons; hence those articles which are of a heavy description are charged at a price seemingly out of all proportion to that of many others which may be obtained at a moderate price: a common grindstone is sold for 20s."[see Note 29]

Now read again the description of Hudson's Bay, discovered by John Hudson in 1610,[see Note 27] then look upon that picture, and upon this; look upon that country that will give eighteen successive crops of wheat, and look upon the difficult, dangerous, and tedious navigation of that bay, whose *climate in summer and winter is horrible*, and through whose waters the stores of this fine country are obliged to travel; look at that picture, then look at this,—the easy, safe, and rapid communication of a Railway,—and say if the time, health and money that would be saved by its construction is not worthy the consideration of Englishmen, and would not repay the constructors, even if that was to be its last terminus.[see Note 54]

But when it is considered that the Main Line of Railway, in passing through our own colonies, would skirt the shores of Lake Superior—rich in mines of silver and copper[see Note 36]—and that the Red River Settlement[see Note 30] would only be one of the many valuable towns and districts that would be opened to trade and commerce, and only contribute its mite to the profits to be obtained from the passage of the Rocky Mountains to the Pacific, it appears to me impossible that such a powerful and wealthy Company as the Hudson's Bay, such magnificent colonies as our North American provinces, and such a power as Great Britain, can balance for one moment in their minds whether loss or profit must attend the undertaking and completion of such a Railway.

[Pg 21] But, vires acquirit eundo, our argument is stronger as we proceed; for, crossing the Rocky Mountains, where the real terminus would be, let us pause for a moment to consider the mine of wealth we should open—not the wealth of gold and silver—but wealth, the reward of commerce and industry.

"The land," Nicolay says, "affords, even now, exports of cattle, wool, hides, and tallow, as well as salted meat, beef, pork, wheat, barley, Indian corn, apples, and timber. Of these all are sent to the Sandwich Islands, some to California, and hides and wool have been sent to England. The woods of the Oregon present another fertile source of national wealth. The growth of timber of all sorts in the neighbourhood of the harbours in the De-fuca Strait adds much to their value as a naval and commercial station. Coal is found in the whole western district, but principally shows itself above the surface on north part of Vancouver's Island. To these sources of commercial and national wealth must be added the minerals—iron, lead, tin, &c. The mountains and seacoast produce granite, slate, sandstone,—and in the interior oolites; limestone is plentiful, and to the north most easily worked and very rich in colour."

Again: look to the whale fishery.[see Note 31] And, in conclusion, we may say that the Hudson's Bay Company's territory in the Pacific, that is, New Caledonia, "will be found to fall short of but a few countries, either in salubrity of climate, fertility of soil, and consequent luxuriance of vegetation, and utility of production, of in the picturesque character of the scenery."

But, my dear friend, I have been led on by my excitement on this subject to make quotations and enter into particulars and details far beyond my original thoughts, which were chiefly to draw the attention of your powerful and active mind to a great national undertaking, knowing well [Pg 22] your love of everything English, and at the same time your devoted attachment to the North American colonies. You have travelled far, and seen much, and have shown in your works how clearly you have observed and appreciated the power and manly spirit of England;

> "Dear for her reputation through the
> world;"

and although you have felt, as a colonist, that her provinces of
North America might have been better governed, and that they
have had even much justly to complain about, still you have always
upheld the connection with England, and argued its value. In writ-
ing to you, the thoughts of old times have returned, and reminded
me of our happy meetings and friendly converse in your lodgings
in Piccadilly; and, thus thinking, I have written on, as in fancy I
have imagined we should have chatted together,—and now I cannot do otherwise than continue in this freedom of communication,
and endeavour to excite you to entertain my thoughts, and to can-
vass them among your fellow-countrymen.

To return, then, to our subject, and to the necessity for England to
be up and stirring. It has been remarked, that "a person who is already thriving seldom puts himself out of his way to commence
even a lucrative improvement, unless urged by the additional motive of fear lest some rival should supplant him by getting possession of it before him." Truly, indeed, has it been said by the Spectator, "that England is not bankrupt, nor poor, nor needy. In every
quarter we see immense additions to material wealth; we observe,
too, on all hands a vast extension of luxurious enjoyments among
the middle classes; every thing attests a huge growth in the wealth
of the nation." It may be fairly considered, then, that England is
thriving—a lucrative improvement of vast magnitude is open to
her—and if the additional motive of fear [Pg 23] of rivalry is necessary to excite her in so noble an undertaking, let her reflect on what
is said in an American paper:—

A Boston paper of the day says, "the finding of these gold mines
is of more importance than any previous event for 300 years. The
prosperity of Queen Elizabeth's reign was mainly owing to the
stimulus given to commerce by the increase of the precious metals;
but the field now to be acted upon is at least fifty times greater than
during that period. Within five years there will be a Railroad from
the Atlantic Ocean, across the great American Continent, through
the gold regions, to the Bay of San Francisco, said to be the finest
harbour in the world. The people of San Francisco will then com-

municate by telegraph in a few minutes, and the mails will be taken to Canton on the one side in fourteen days, and to London on the other in nine days; so that intelligence may be conveyed from the one end to the other in the short period of twenty-three days. This will be witnessed under five years."

It is evident, then, that the people of the United States are quite aware of all the advantages to be gained by a quick communication across the Continent of America. Let us consider now, for a moment, what the consequences of a railway would be as regards your own valuable and fertile colonies.[see Note 43]

You have no doubt already pictured to yourself the town of Halifax alive with all the bustle and excitement of a great commercial community, and her noble harbours full of every description of vessels, from the magnificent English steamer to the small colonial coasting craft; for soon, not merely one steamer a week, as now, would touch from England on her way to New York, but Nova Scotia herself, from [Pg 24] the increasing wealth and importance of her towns, would require the use of many steamers to enable her to carry on the numerous commercial duties that would fall to her lot; and when we reflect that at Halifax would rest the terminus, whence could be embarked for England at all seasons of the year our highly valuable colonial produce, including the rich exports from the Southern Pacific Ocean (not sent round Cape Horn or the Cape of Good Hope); and when we reflect that this long neglected seaport town could equally receive at all seasons of the year the various exports from England, for her numerous Colonies; and when we consider that there is abundance of coal at hand, with wood and stone for building, who can hesitate for a moment to acknowledge that Halifax would soon become one of the most important ports, and one of the most noble cities of the world; add to this, that the connection and attachment of Nova Scotia to England would be cemented for ever — and that the dream of the Clockmaker would be realized. "This is the best situation in all America — is Nova Scotia, if the British did but know it. It will have the greatest trade, the greatest population, the most manufactures, the most wealth, of any state this side of the water. The resources, natural advantages, and political position of this place, beats all." Then again, look to the city of Quebec; no sooner would the river navigation be open than thousands of vessels from England would be seen dropping their anchors at the foot of her proud citadel, carrying out vast cargoes of English exports; then picture to yourself the railway terminus, alive with all the consequent bustle, the steam up, and the railway carriages ready to convey all these articles of commerce to every town and district in the North American Colonies; away also to the far west, whence they would be forwarded to our colonial possessions in the Southern Pacific, and to numerous other places; then [Pg 25] again, behold these ships reloading quickly with the timber and other exportable articles from our then firmly-linked-together valuable Colonies, sailing away for England, and repeating their visit two or three times in the season; the difficult navigation of the Hudson's Bay avoided; the territory of the Hudson's Bay Company daily increasing in value, from the ease with which its inhabitants could procure articles of commerce, before almost forbidden to them; and Quebec, being their nearest port for embarkation for England, would necessarily become even a much more important city than she is at present. The land in her neighbourhood would become highly valuable, and, as a matter of necessity, the fine country to the north, with even better soil and better climate, would soon be opened and peopled. I cannot cease referring to Quebec without recording my gratitude for many kindnesses there received—particularly from the family of Captain Boxer.[see Note 55] Then again, look to New Brunswick, connected as it would of course be both with Halifax and Quebec, thus, having a free and direct communication with those cities, and enabled to export or import at any season of the year, (should she wish to avoid the navigation of the Bay of Fundy); then think what strength she would bring to the union of the Colonies by such a link of connection, and how many more opportunities her inhabitants would have of encouraging and fostering that strong attachment to their English brethren we all so well know to exist amongst the people of New Brunswick.

But, my dear friend, I might go on this way for ever, pointing out town after town, and district after district, showing how the wealth and prosperity of each would go on rapidly increasing. I cannot, however, quit the subject without a passing word on Montreal, in which city I have [Pg 26] passed many happy days, and from whose inhabitants I have received much kindness and civility. That noble city has already made some steady advances to a great capital, and the time cannot be far distant when she will rival even the most flourishing on the North American Continent. To her this proposed Railway would be highly important. She has shown that she already understands the value of such things; for not only has she a small one of her own to La-Chine, about seven miles up the river, but she has also, I understand, finished about thirty miles towards the Atlantic in the direction of Portland. The interest of these Companies would not of course be lost sight of, but their profits taken into the general calculation. The great Trunk Line of Railway would naturally, I conclude, go through a country some distance to the north of Montreal; but one of the most important termini must of necessity be at that city where the business of the Government is carried on, and where of course a general Railway Communication with every town and district would be established. Toronto would naturally be considered in the manner in which so loyal and devoted a city ought to be, and where was held, even to a very late period, the parliament of a great country, surrendered only to her sister Montreal on public considerations and for the general good;[see Note 62] and the Main Line of Railway should be brought as near Toronto as the communication between the Atlantic and Pacific (its great object and principal view) would permit. Hamilton, Kingston, Byetown and several other places must not consider themselves neglected, if not herein specially mentioned; but in fact as regards these Colonies, the song of your friend, the Clockmaker, about them cannot be sung too often. "Oh Squire! if John Bull only knew the value of these Colonies, he would be a great [Pg 27] man, I tell you,—but he don't." Truly do I hope that I may now sing to them with confidence,—

> "There's a good time coming yet,
> Wait a little longer."

In your conversation with the Clockmaker you have observed, "it is painful to think of the blunders that have been committed from time to time in the management of our Colonies, and of the gross ignorance or utter disregard of their interests that has been displayed in treaties with foreign powers. Fortunately for the Mother Country, the Colonists are warmly attached to her and her institutions, and deplore a separation too much to agitate questions, however important, that may have a tendency to weaken their affections by arousing their passions." Should the Government of Great Britain, upon whose consideration will be forced the present situation of her Colonies, consider it right to give their support to this proposed Atlantic and Pacific Railway for the reasons herein explained, or from any other cause,—the great benefit that Nova Scotia, New Brunswick and the Canadas will derive from having open to them a free and easy access to the Atlantic and the Pacific, will, I trust, occasion such an activity of mind and such an employment of matter, that in the general good arising therefrom, all thoughts of former ill treatment or unkindness from the Mother Country will soon be forgotten.

The great question, however, is, and will be on all sides, Where is the money to come from?[see Note 56] and that question I am weak enough to fancy is easily answered. Let us consider this subject a little. Let us remember, first, that England expended 630 millions during nineteen years in war, and, notwithstanding which expenditure, the country got richer [Pg 28] and richer every day;[see Note 14] and if the country is not poorer now than it was in the years when it was able to raise the sum of 150 millions in a single year—the greater part of which it could afford to expend in one year in war, and grow richer all the time—surely such a country can afford to expend some few millions for the benefit of those colonies on account of whom she was lately ready to go to war, and on whose account she did actually expend about two millions, caused merely by the rebellion and disturbance of a few discontented spirits. But the money that England would be called upon to advance in the proposed undertaking would secure to her not only the attachment of her children in the North American provinces, by making it as well their worldly interest, as it is their natural feeling and wish, to remain Englishmen; but that money, and the interest of that money, could be secured to her by proper arrangements being entered into with the Hudson's Bay Company, and with the North American provinces, and be ultimately reimbursed to her by the formation of the proposed Company.

Up to the present moment England has, I believe, only expended the sum of £148,000,000 on her Railways, and, I believe, nearly 5000 miles are finished; and on an average these Railways are said to give a return of about four per cent., and "with the increase of the national wealth and population, and with the increase of habits of social inter-communication and the transit of goods, the traffic on Railways would increase, and the profits and dividends would not be less but greater; and in the case of some of them, no man would pretend to say how great might be the increase of dividends from the improved and economical modes of working Railways, which, there is every reason to believe, will day by day be freshly discovered." [*Bradshaw's Almanack, 1849*]. [Pg 29] And who will say that £200,000,000 expended (even should such a sum as that be required) in making a Railway Road from the Atlantic to the Pacific through our own territories, and therefore completely under our own controul, would not increase by a tenfold degree the value of that property already expended in England? When the Railways now in contemplation at home are finished, their total length will, I believe, be about 10,000 miles, and the expenditure between 200 and 240 millions. The length of the Railway proposed to go through our colonies may be spoken of roughly as at about 4000 miles; but when we take into consideration the relative value of land in England and our colonies, and a thousand other Railway contingencies in a highly civilized country, creating enormous legal, legislative and other expenses, we naturally come to the conclusion that the outlay per mile must of course be considerably diminished in the colonies. Taking it, however, at the English expenditure of £24,000 a mile on the average, it would only cost £96,000,000;[see Note 32]— £5,000,000 has been estimated as sufficient for six hundred miles of Railway from Halifax to Quebec. But calling it £100,000,000, and supposing the work to be five years completing, that would only be at the rate of £20,000,000 a year, the interest of which at five per cent. would be £1,000,000. Surely, then, such a sum as that could be easily raised, even by the Hudson's Bay Company alone, upon the security of their extensive and valuable territory. For so great a difference would soon arise between the value of that territory as it is now—merely the abode of Indians and hunters—and what it would be then; with its clearings, its improvements, its roads, its trade, its manufactures, and its towns, that any amount of debt almost might be incurred. But our loyal colonies would no doubt equally enter into securities to England, and [Pg 30] be glad, in fact, to share their chance of the profit; for these colonies, as well as the Hudson's Bay Company, would be immense gainers. Still it may be argued, that unless it can be shown that England herself would be a gainer, she would not be justified in advancing any money on such an undertaking. Let us, then, consider this point a little. Mr. Cobden has asserted (what some of our public journals confess to be true), "that if the revenue had fallen off, it was because the balance sheet of the merchants and the manufacturers had fallen off likewise." If then we show by the undertaking of such a work as is now proposed, the balance sheets of the merchants and manufacturers must increase immensely, we surely make out a case for the good of the country generally, as far as revenue is concerned.

Let us then first consider, that "So interwoven and complicated are the fibres which form the texture of the highly civilized and artificial community in which we live, that an effect produced on any one point is instantly transmitted to the most remote and apparently unconnected parts of the system." And again—"The exportation of labourers and capital from the old to the new countries, from a place where their productive power is less to a place where it is greater, increases by so much the aggregate produce of the labour and capital of the world."

Now, with regard to the first remark, the effect that would be produced by the necessary exportation of all the machinery for the making and working of this Atlantic and Pacific Railway, would of course produce, even in England, a very great increase both to the productive power and to the consumption of a variety of articles apparently unconnected with the affairs of the Railway; and when, again, we look to the necessary exportation of labourers and of capital to the towns on the Line of the [Pg 31] Railway where there is less productive power at work, by increasing that dormant power we shall increase the aggregate capital of the world, and consequently that of England. Again—"Could we suddenly double the productive power of the country, we should double the supply of the commodities in every market, but we should by the same stroke double the purchasing power—every body would bring a double demand as well as supply—every body would be able to buy twice as much, as he would have twice as much to offer in exchange." Also—"A country which produces for a larger market than its own, can introduce a more extended division of labour—can make a greater use of machinery, and is more likely to make inventions and improvements in the progress of production." Again—"Whatever causes a greater quantity of any thing to be produced in the same place, tends to the general increase of the productive powers of the world." Now it surely will not be denied, that the undertaking of this National Railway would cause in England a greater quantity of machinery to be made and exported to the North American provinces, thus producing for it a larger market than the home, and causing a greater quantity to be made—thus a general increase of the productive powers of the world must be produced; and as "wealth may be defined as all useful or agreeable things which possess exchangeable value," it necessarily follows that the immense increase that would be given to the productive powers of England, to those of her North American provinces, and of the Hudson's Bay territory, by an undertaking on such an extensive scale, if it did not completely, would nearly double these powers; and as whoever brings additional commodities to market brings additional power to purchase, it follows that the inhabitants of our North American provinces, and of the Hudson's [Pg 32] Bay territory, would be enabled to take nearly twice the quantity of our manufactured goods.

Lord Stanley, in moving an amendment to the Address from the Throne, says: "the exports of the six principal articles of British industry, cotton, wool, linen, silk, hardware and earthenware, exhibit a diminution as compared with 1847, of no less than four millions, and as compared with 1846, of five millions;" such being the case, it becomes highly important to consider the cause of this falling off, with a view to a remedy, and some great measures must be adopted towards our own colonies that will enable them to receive a greater quantity of manufactured goods from the mother country,—and this great Railway is suggested as one that would increase the productive power and population of our North American colonies, and a consequent increasing necessity for hardware and earthenware, to say nothing even of the other articles of British industry, or of the facility of communicating with our other Colonies.

These few remarks will suffice to show that the balance sheets of the merchants, and consequently of the revenue of England, as well as the capital of individuals, must increase immensely during the construction of and at the completion of the proposed undertaking. Mr. Montgomery Martin has stated that "Railways are the very grandest organization of labour and capital that the world has ever seen:" that "the capital actually invested in Railways advanced from £65,000,000 in 1843 to £167,000,000 in 1848—no less than £100,000,000 in five years." And why should we not look forward to an equal—aye—and to a much larger investment—on such a magnificent Line of Railway? joining, as it would, all the northern dominions of the old world—crossing, as it would, the northern territories of the new, and making an easy opening to the rich and thriving world that may be [Pg 33] considered of the present day. For "the word has been given, an active and enterprising population will be poured in, every element of progress will be cultivated, and the productive countries on the shores of the Pacific, heretofore isolated, will be brought into active and profitable intercourse. It may truly be said that a new world has been opened.

"Our fathers watched the progress of America, we ourselves have seen that of Australia, but the opening of the Pacific is one of the greatest events in social history since, in the fifteenth century, the East Indies were made known to Europe; for we have not, as in America or Australia, to await the slow growth of European settlements, but to witness at once the energetic action of countries already in a high state of advancement. The Eastern and the Western shores of the great Ocean will now be brought together as those of the Atlantic are, and will minister to each other's wants. A happy coincidence of circumstances has prepared the way for these results. Everything was ready, the word only was wanted to begin, and it has been given.

"The outflowings of Chinese emigrants and produce, which have gone towards the East, will now move to the West; the commercial enterprise of Australia and New Zealand has acquired a new field of exercise and encouragement; the markets which Chili and Peru have found in Europe only, will be opened nearer to their doors; the north-west shore of America will obtain all the personal and material means of organization; the Islands of the Pacific will take the place in the career of civilization for which the labours of the missionary have prepared them; and even Japan will not be able to withhold itself from the community of nations.

"This is worth more to our merchants and manufacturers, and to the people employed by them, than even [Pg 34] the gold mines can be; for this is the statement of certain results, and the working of the gold mines, however productive they may prove, must be attended with all the incidents of irregularity and uncertainty, and great commercial disadvantages." — (*Wyld's Geographical Notes.*)

Surely then there would be no difficulty with Parliament to encourage and facilitate the formation of an Atlantic and Pacific Railway Company, by obtaining its sanction to the loan of £150,000,000 in such sums as might be required (to be issued under the sanction of a board appointed for that special purpose), particularly when it is recollected that the expense of the greater part of her own convicts could be provided for by that advance.

It will easily be seen that it would be impossible to complete this Atlantic and Pacific Railway, without at the same time giving great encouragement to the emigration of labour; and this "is only practicable when its cost is defrayed *or at least advanced by others*, than the labourers themselves. Who then is to advance it? Naturally it may be said, the capitalists of the colony, who require the labour, and who intend to profit by it. But to this there is the obstacle, that a capitalist, after going to the expense of carrying out labourers, has no security that he shall be the person to derive any benefit from them." To those who would object to Government interference in a case like the present, we can only say, in the words of Mr. Mill, that "the question of Government intervention in the work of colonization involves the future and permanent interests of civilization itself, and far outstretches the comparatively narrow limits of purely economical considerations; but, even with a view to these considerations alone, the removal of population from the overcrowded to the unoccupied parts of the earth's surface, is one of those works of eminent [Pg 35] social usefulness which most require, and which at the same time will best repay, the intervention of Government." "No individual or body of individuals *could* reimburse themselves for these expenses." Government, on the contrary, *could* take from the increasing wealth *caused by the construction of this Railway and consequent great emigration, the fraction which would suffice to repay with interest the money advanced.* These remarks apply equally to the governments of the North American provinces as to those of the Hudson's Bay Company and Great Britain. [see Note 57]

Let us now personify our Atlantic and Pacific Railway, and endeavour more immediately to apply some of the reasoning as regards colonization to the money part of the question as regards the Railway. As regards colonization the question—Who is to advance the money? has, I think, been very clearly answered by Mr. Mill. As regards the undertaking of this Railway, and the answer to the question, Where is the money to come from? let us first suppose then that "there is an increase of the quantity of money, caused by the arrival of a foreigner in a place with a treasure of gold and silver; when he commences expending it, he adds to the supply of money and by the same act to the demand for goods. If he expends his funds in establishing a manufactory, he will raise the price of labour and materials; but, at the higher prices, more money will pass into the hands of the sellers of these different articles; and they, whether labourers or dealers, having more money to lay out, will create an increased demand for all things which they are accustomed to purchase, and these accordingly will rise in price, and so on, until the rise has reached every thing." Now let us for a moment suppose this foreigner to be represented by our friend the Atlantic and Pacific Railway, (imagined, for the sake of our argument, to be completed), and we will no longer consider him a foreigner, but a brother. [Pg 36] This brother, on his arrival in England finds that he has unfortunately forgotten to bring with him his purse, that in fact he has neither gold nor silver, the representatives of wealth, and here, be it remembered, that wealth is any thing useful or agreeable, and that money is a commodity. We will then suppose this North American brother to say, My good brother of England, I am here without gold or silver, or without any kind of wealth; the commodities I have left behind me are of such a nature, that without much labour I could not put them in such a shape as would enable me to bring them to this country, nor could I obtain silver or gold enough to represent them; unless, therefore, I send some labouring people and machinery to my country, I am afraid I cannot obtain all the commodities I wish to have. Now you have plenty of spare labourers, and plenty of spare machinery and other useful materials, and for which you would be glad to receive valuable commodities in my country; and if you will only send the labourers and machinery out, I will order that in return you shall be allowed to bring away all the useful and agreeable things, that is, all the wealth that may be found, and have the use of such things as you may prefer to keep in my country. Now if you will make this agreement with me, I will return with you to my native land, and will not only assist you to obtain all these commodities, but I will engage also to pay you a certain annual income out of my saving; and I will show you the short way to the most extensive region of wealth ever known to any nation in the world; and you can then travel that road, so that at no future period (at least within the imagination of man) shall you ever again complain of too great a population on your soil, or too small a market for your labour.

Then the good brother of England says to this Atlantic and Pacific brother,—We believe all you say of your [Pg 37] wealth, and we see the great advantage it would be to us to partake of it, and to have the command of the road you point out, but what security are we to have that when our labourers and machinery are sent to your country they will be employed; and if you have neither gold nor silver nor other commodities ready to give us in exchange for the work and the articles, how are we to pay the people to prepare the machinery, and all our other labourers, whose wages would in England of course become higher, as they would be less in number, and there would be a greater quantity of work to be done. The brothers, in talking over this matter, discovered that "credit is indispensable, for rendering the whole capital of the country productive. It is also the means by which the industrial talent of the country is turned to most account for purposes of production. Many a person who has no capital of his own, or very little, but who has qualifications for business, which are known and appreciated by some person of capital, is enabled to obtain either advances of money, or more frequently goods, on credit, by which his industrial capacities are made instrumental in the increase of public wealth." The Pacific and Atlantic brother observed,—This is exactly my case. Only give me credit, and I will bind myself on my own personal security to give up whatever portion of my annual income you may consider necessary; and I will also secure the money advanced by you on my land, on the minerals thereof, and in any other way that may be deemed necessary. My brother of the Atlantic and Pacific Railway, says the Englishman, you have nearly convinced me; we will immediately appoint friends to draw up all the necessary agreements between us, that will enable me, if possible, to advance you such labour and machinery as may be required; and we will also proceed to appoint other friends, who shall take into consideration, in the first place, the expense incurred from your birth to a state [Pg 38] of manhood, and the annual income that is derived from your business and your property; and leaving you sufficient to maintain yourself as a gentleman, we shall appropriate to ourselves whatever may remain, as a reward for our exertions and the risk to be incurred, and as a security for the interest of the money expended upon your account. The brothers having thus agreed in a general way, proceed immediately to appoint friends and to call upon their good old mother, Great Britain, to advance the money required, and their North American relations, Nova Scotia, New Brunswick, Canada, and Hudson's Bay, to come forward and make a general family treaty for the security and payment of such advances. The brothers were then congratulating themselves on what they considered the success of their project, when it was whispered to them that something of a similar plan had been proposed for their relation Ireland, by one "whose loss is too great to be slighted, and too recent not to be felt;" and it had been suggested that for every £100 expended on Railways in that country, £200 should be lent by Government; upon which occasion it had been observed by one who has greatly influenced, whether for good or evil, will be hereafter known, the destinies of the British Empire, that "the public credit of the State is one of the elements of our financial strength, and that it was not possible to appropriate a great portion of that public credit to the encouragement of commercial enterprises, without, to the same extent, foregoing the power to apply that public credit in another direction, in the event of the national exigencies requiring you to do so." The brothers replied, this is certainly true; but the proposed undertaking is not a commercial enterprise, although no doubt it would produce great commercial and colonizing results; but it is a grand national work,—a desideratum that has been wished for, looked for, and cared for, ever since the new world was discovered—that has repeatedly called forth great [Pg 39] expenditure of money, great suffering, and loss of life in searching for it, to the north. It is, in short, the great high road between the Atlantic and Pacific—the expense of making which you are called upon to consider.

As regards Ireland, another bold measure has been suggested for that country; without giving any opinion upon it, I cannot help asking why we should not be as bold in peace as we were in war. Must we wait until

> "The news is, sir, the Voices are in
> arms;
> *Then indeed*—we shall have means to
> vent
> Our musty superfluity?"

"Without raising one shilling out of the Exchequer," says Lucius (see *Morning Post, Jan. 31st*), "boldly apply the national credit to relieve the national distress; at once authorize the Bank of Ireland, or a bank to be created for that purpose, to issue twenty or thirty millions in aid of the landed proprietors; secondly, for the judicious encouragement of emigration, transplant those who cannot earn a subsistence at home to a comfortable settlement in our colonies, and to promote such mercantile or other undertakings, let the notes issued be made legal tenders for all payments whatever, and let the entire soil of Ireland be pledged for their ultimate security." Far be it from me to give any opinion on what is best to be done for Ireland, but certain I feel that what is here proposed and suggested regarding an Atlantic and Pacific Railway could not interfere with any plan Government might think right to adopt for the regeneration of Ireland, unless indeed by greatly facilitating all emigration plans and permanent employment.

But, independently of all this money question, "there is the strongest obligation on the government of a country like our own, with a crowded population and unoccupied continents under its command, to build as it were and keep open a bridge from the mother country to those continents." Let us reflect that "the economical advantages [Pg 40] of commerce are surpassed in importance by those of its effects, which are intellectual and moral. It is hardly possible to overrate the value, for the improvement of human beings, of things which bring them in contact with persons dissimilar to themselves, and with modes of thought and action unlike those with which they are familiar. Commerce is now what war once was—the principal source of this contact. Commercial adventurers from more advanced countries have generally been the first civilizers of barbarians, and commerce is the purpose of the far greater part of the communication which takes place between civilized nations. It is commerce which is rapidly rendering war obsolete, by strengthening and multiplying the personal interest which is in natural opposition to it." — (*Mill, Polit. Econ.*) In whatever point of view, therefore, we regard this subject—whether as one of duty by providing the means of healthy and legitimate employment to our numerous artificers and labourers now in a state of destitution—a domestic calamity likely to be often inflicted upon us— unless new fields, easy of access, are made permanently open to our continually increasing population—and "it would be difficult to show that it is not as much the duty of rulers to provide, as far as they can, for the removal of a domestic calamity, as it is to guard the people entrusted to their care from foreign outrage"—will they "slumber till some great emergency, some dreadful economic or other crisis, reveals the capacities of evil which the volcanic depths of our society may now hide under but a deep crust?"—or whether we view it as a means of assisting any general system in the penal code—or whether we view it as a point of individual or government interest, by turning all that extra-productive power, now idle, in the direction of our own colonies, and thus connecting and attaching them more strongly to the mother country—increasing their [Pg 41] wealth, their power and our own:—or whether we consider it in a moral and religious point of view, as affording greater and quicker facilities for the spread of education and the Gospel of Christ[see Note 58]—or whether we look upon it as an instrument for the increase of commerce, and (as an important consequence) the necessarily directing men's minds, with the bright beams of hope from their own individual and immediate distress, as well as from the general excitement and democratic feeling and spirit of contention showing itself amongst many nations (an object greatly to be desired) for—

> "The times are wild....
> ....Every minute now
> *May* be the father of some stratagem;"

—or whether we look at it in a political point of view, as keeping open to us at all times, without the necessity of interference with other nations or of war, a great high road to most of our colonial possessions, and particularly to India—viewing it then in any one of these points, who can doubt for a moment the beneficial results that must attend such an undertaking. But when all these considerations are taken together, we must repeat what we said in a former page, that it is a grand and a noble undertaking, and that it must be accomplished by Great Britain and her colonies.

Let us reflect, lastly, my dear friend, that "the world now contains several extensive regions, provided with various ingredients of wealth, in a degree of abundance of which former ages had not even an idea." Your native land, and the other North American provinces, have, even by their own exertions, made rapid advances in wealth, accompanied by moral and intellectual attainments, and can look forward at no very distant period (if even left to their own exertions) to be enabled to take a very prominent position in the affairs of the world. [Pg 42] But the Hudson's Bay Company's territory is still nearly in its primitive state, and much indeed is to be expected from its advancement, when it shall have taken its proper station in the general trade and commerce of mankind; the position of Vancouver's Island is such that there is little reason to doubt its wealth and consequence will place it high in the scale of England's offspring.[see Note 59]

But, my dear friend, unless your mind has become as fully impressed as my own with the vast importance of this great Railway undertaking, I shall only tire you the more and detain you to no purpose by dwelling longer on the subject; and indeed even should your mind be satisfied with the importance of the work, it may yet conceive it to be of an impracticable nature. "Who (I have been asked) in the living generation would be reimbursed for the outlay? and without that, who will undertake a national work, however grand or remunerative to future ages?" To this I answer fearlessly, that thousands of human beings of the present generation would benefit by the outlay; that the employment would be a quite sufficiently lucrative one and visibly so, as to induce the English capitalist to come forward and undertake the formation of a Company; for even at this moment Railways are in contemplation,[see Note 40] if not actually commenced, from Halifax to Quebec and from New Brunswick to Halifax; and how much more would these Lines be paying Lines when they had also an opening to the Pacific! But no individual nor combination of individuals could have sufficient influence with, or, if they had the influence, could have the necessary power to induce, the Hudson's Bay Company to open its territories, and to enter into all the arrangements and all the agreements that would be necessary to be made with that Company, with England, and with the North American [Pg 43] Colonies, before a work affecting the interests of so many could be commenced.

It is necessary then that Government should take the initiative, and it is not uncommon for her so to do in all great national works, such as roads, surveys, expeditions either for the objects of science or commerce; such as those sent to discover the north-west passage, upon which thousands have been spent,[see Note 44] and on account of which, at this very moment, England has to deplore, in all probability, the loss of many a noble son, whose relatives have been for so long a time kept in all the agony of suspense. Upon no other description of work would Great Britain be required to advance a single penny; but the very fact of her undertaking what may be considered legitimate expenses of a government, the survey and marking out the whole Line, the entering into treaties with her Colonies and the Hudson's Bay Company for the general security of the money, and for the interest for a certain number of years of the capital of the Company, would give such a confidence to the public mind, that a very short time would bring into full operation in that direction, sufficient of the power and wealth of England to accomplish the work; and when accomplished, Government would still hold a lien upon it until she was reimbursed every penny. And, let me ask, are there not a thousand expenditures that have been undertaken by Government for which no reimbursement has ever taken place; and are not individuals every day risking their capital and their accumulation of savings, in speculations in foreign lands,[see Note 61] when the result of those past connections have been such as to lead the Minister of Foreign Affairs, even in his place in the House of Commons, to hold out as it were a threat to the whole world, if England's children did not receive their due. Surely it would be more prudent, more politically [Pg 44] wise, and more economical, for Government to encourage the expenditure of our own capital in our own Colonies.

Sitting in his arm chair, in his office in London, the Minister of Great Britain can now convey his thoughts, his wishes, his commands, in a few moments to every part of England and Scotland, and will soon be enabled to do so to Ireland.[see Note 66] He can send the soldiers, horse and foot, as well as the artillery of Great Britain, flying through the land at almost any rate he wishes. And all heavy stores and goods of the merchants can be easily forwarded at about twopence, and even, I believe, a penny a mile per ton, and at about twenty miles an hour; and a penny a letter now enables every individual in England to communicate, at almost every hour, with his distant friends and relations; the post office itself travelling at a rate and with an ease little to be comprehended by those who have not witnessed it. The result of such immense wealth and such enormous power is more than is required for England, and would necessarily carry with it its own destruction, was not her empire one which encircles the world.

Let the minister then who guides and directs the wealth and power above described, and in whose hands the destinies and happiness of thousands are placed, picture to himself the encouragement that would be given to British industry and British enterprize, if, at ten days distance from her shores, a port was established from which he would be enabled to send across the Continent of America his thoughts, his wishes, and his commands, with the same speed at which they now travel throughout England; and if these thoughts, wishes and commands would reach every one of our own Colonies in the Pacific in about fifteen days after leaving the western shore of North America; and if from the same port (ten days distance from England) could also be despatched the troops of Great Britain, if unfortunately necessary, travelling at the rate [Pg 45] before described; if heavy stores and merchants' goods could also be enabled to cross the Continent of America, at the same price and at the same speed as they now travel in England; if the post office system could also be introduced, and if letters at a penny each might pass between relation and relation, between friend and friend from England to her most distant Colonies—if her children gone forth to colonize could then either return or communicate their every wish to England in less than a month; and reclining in his own arm chair, reflecting as he ought to do and must do upon the power and wealth of England, let him not say that all here described is not easily within her reach. Let him rather consider the subject with a view to become the Leader of the Country in such a noble work. If it is a bold work, let him remember that fortune favours the brave. — "Si secuta fuerit, quod debet Fortuna, gaudebimus omnes, sin minus, ego tamen gaudebo."

And now, my dear friend, whose patience I have so long taxed, it is time that we should part —

> "Whether we shall meet
> again I know not;
> If we do meet again —
> why we shall smile.
> If not, for ever and for
> ever farewell."

Believe me,

sincerely and faithfully attached,

ROBERT CARMICHAEL-SMYTH.

Junior United Service Club,
*February, 1849.*

[Pg 46]

# CONCLUSION.

The last correction for the press was scarcely finished, when "Canada in 1848" was put into my hands. Had I, a month ago, seen that little pamphlet, written as it is with so much spirit and ability, I should hardly, perhaps, have felt sufficiently inclined to have suggested one Line of Railway, in opposition to the views of its talented author. I trust I need scarcely assure Lieut. Synge, that in any observations I have made upon Canals, I had no reference whatever to his grand scheme,—nor the least intention of treating lightly his magnificent project, of which, until a day or two ago, I did not even know the existence. I cannot now, however, let my Letter to my friend the Author of the Clockmaker go forth to the public, without availing myself of the opportunity thus afforded me, of bringing also to the notice of those who read that letter "the existing resources of British North America," so fully and powerfully pointed out by Lieut. Millington Henry Synge, of the Royal Engineers. Educated myself at Woolwich, and having served for seven years in his sister corps, the Artillery, I feel proud and happy that there are so many points upon which we can and do agree. There are some, however, and one in particular most important, on which we are completely at issue. Lieut. Synge says, "A ship annually arrives at Fort York for the service of the Hudson's Bay Company; who can tell how many may eventually do so?" Now my wish is that the one "annually" arriving may never have again to travel that Bay, *whose climate in winter and summer is [Pg 47] horrible.* I shall say no more on this subject at present; but I strongly recommend all those who have condescended to read and reflect upon the foregoing pages, to read and reflect also upon what has been written by Lieut. Synge. His pamphlet has afforded me the greatest possible pleasure. The manner in which (p. 5) he speaks of the people of the Colonies is completely in unison with my own expressed feelings; and all the arguments that he brings forward in favour of the great work upon which he has evidently thought so much, and in his pamphlet so clearly explained, bear equally in favour of the suggested Railway. He states that there is "a field open to almost an illimitable capital of labour; that the systematic development of the resources of British North America will, so far from being a drain upon Great Britain, be of immediate advantage to her. That such development entails a natural, enduring, and perfect union between Great Britain and that part of her empire in North America. That completeness of communication, including facility, rapidity, and security, is indeed the true secret of the rapidity and completeness of the development of the country." These are the thoughts of Lieut. Synge, and I think I have already explained that they are equally mine. We have suggested different methods. Lieut. Synge wishes to improve the old Line of water communication; and Colonization would then be naturally confined to the banks of Rivers and of Lakes. A great Line of Railway communication would, on the other hand, be naturally of some distance from the River, and in many instances carried through the heart of the country, and thus serve as another main artery, in which would circulate the wealth of the empire, and on each side of which would be opened valuable land, on which settlers could locate without being lost, or disheartened by the solitude of the wilderness. Again, Lieut. Synge asks, "Is it not [Pg 48] wonderful that no independent mail route exists, to give the British Provinces the benefit of the geographical position of Halifax. Is it not wonderful that there should be no interprovincial means of rapid communication?" Such are the questions of Lieut. Synge—and such questions, I trust, will soon be answered by a Colonial Minister—that a new era will soon be open for the Colonies—new life and energy be given to them. But time presses, and I must here conclude, with again assuring Lieut. Synge of the sincere pleasure with which I have read his pamphlet, and that I shall make use of such extracts as can be hastily added, in the shape of Notes, to my own Letter to the Author of the Clockmaker:—happy shall I be if we agree—

> "Sul campo della gloria
> noi pugneremo a lato:
> Frema o sorrida il fato
> vicino a te starò,
> La morte o la vittoria con
> te dividero."

ROBERT CARMICHAEL-SMYTH.

Junior United Service Club,
*February 28, 1849.*

[Pg 49]

# NOTES.

(1) The writer of this letter, when returning from Halifax to England in the spring of 1838, had the good fortune to take his passage in the same government packet with the author of the Clockmaker, who was proceeding to England with the second series of that work: and afterwards, when paying a momentary visit to Halifax in the winter of 1844, he experienced the high gratification of knowing, by the very kind reception he met with, that he had not been forgotten neither, by his Compagnons de voyage, Haliburton and Howe, nor by the other kind and highly valued friends he had formerly made in that city.

(2) The history and particulars of this canal are well known at Halifax, and Samuel P. Fairbanks, Esq. (Master of the Rolls at Nova Scotia) brought to England with him in the Tyrian all the plans, maps, &c. connected with that canal, and was, I believe, sent as a representative of the parties connected with the work, in the hope that he might be able to induce the government to advance sufficient money for its completion. The fine large locks of this canal remain to tell the tale of money sunk in an unfinished work. No encouragement certainly to canal speculations.

(3) "The distance, as I make it, from Bristol to New York Lighthouse, is 3037 miles; from Bristol to Halifax Lighthouse is 2479; from Halifax Light to New York Light is 522 miles, in all 3001 miles; 558 miles shorter than New York Line, and even going to New York 36 miles shorter to stop at Halifax, than go to New York direct." — So says the Clockmaker in 1838.

(4) "Get your legislatur' to persuade Government to contract with the Great Western folks to carry the mail, and drop it in their way to New York; for you got as much and as good coal to Nova Scotia as England has, and the steam boats would have to carry a supply of 550 miles less, and could take in a stock at Halifax for the return voyage to Europe. If ministers won't do that, get 'em to send steam packets of their own, and you wouldn't be no longer an everlastin' outlandish country no more as you be now. And, more than that, you wouldn't lose all the best emigrants and all their capital." — *Clockmaker, 1838.*

[Pg 50] (5) "The communication by steam between Nova Scotia and England will form a new era in colonial history. It will draw closer the bonds of affection between the two countries, afford a new and extended field for English capital, and develope the resources of that valuable but neglected province. Mr. Slick, with his usual vanity, claims the honour of suggesting it, as well as the merit of having, by argument and ridicule, reasoned and shamed the Government into its adoption." — *Clockmaker, 1841.*

(6) "In the Duke of Kent the Nova Scotians lost a kind patron and a generous friend. The loyalty of the people, which, when all America was revolting, remained firm and unshaken, and the numerous proofs he received of their attachment to their king and to himself, made an impression upon his mind that was neither effaced nor weakened by time or distance. Should these pages happily meet the eye of a colonial minister, who has other objects in view than the security of place and the interest of a party, may they remind him of a duty that has never been performed but by the illustrious individual, whose former residence among us gave rise to these reflections. This work is designed for the cottage, and not for the palace; and the author has not the presumption even to hope that it can ever be honoured by the perusal of his sovereign. Had he any ground for anticipating such a distinction for it, he would avail himself of this opportunity of mentioning that, in addition to the dutiful affection the Nova Scotians have always borne to their monarch, they feel a more lively interest in, and a more devoted attachment to, the present occupant of the throne, from the circumstance of the long and close connexion that subsisted between them and her illustrious parent. He was their patron, benefactor and friend. To be a Nova Scotian was of itself a sufficient passport to his notice, and to posses merit a sufficient guarantee for his favour. Her Majesty reigns therefore, in this little province, in the hearts of her subjects, a dominion of love inherited from her father." — *Clockmaker, 1841.*

"It can hardly be said that England has hitherto drawn any positive advantages from the possession of these provinces, if we place out of view the conveniences afforded during periods of war by the harbour of Halifax. But the negative advantage from them are evident, if we consider that the United Slates of America are greatly deficient in good harbours on the Atlantic coast, while Nova Scotia possesses, in addition to the magnificent harbour of Halifax, eleven ports, between it and Cape Canso, with sufficient depth of water for the largest ships of war." — *Clockmaker, 1841.*

[Pg 51] (7) "The necessity which is gradually developing itself for steam fleets in the Pacific, will open a mine of wealth to the inhabitants of the West Coast of America." — *Rev. C. G. Nicolay, 1846.*

The same author, in speaking of the principal features of the Iron Bound Coast and Western Archipelago, in the centre of Vancouver's Island, the Straits of Fuca and Puget's Inlet, says, "Its maritime importance is entirely confined to the Strait of Juan de Fuca and southern extremity of Vancouver's Island. Here are presented a series of harbours unrivalled in quality and capacity, at least within the same limits; and here, as has been remarked, it is evident the future emporium of the Pacific, in West America will be found." And now that it has been settled that this magnificent strait and its series of harbours (this great emporium of West America) is open to that great and enterprising nation, the people of the United States, as well as to ourselves, it becomes most important to us that we should, and quickly, open the best possible and shortest road to communicate with it.

"Alexander Mackenzie, who had risen to the station of a partner in that Company, and was even among them remarkable for his energy and activity both of body and mind, having, with others of the leading partners, imbibed very extensive views of the commercial importance and capabilities of Canada, and considering that the discovery of a passage by sea from the Atlantic to the Pacific would contribute greatly to open, and enlarge it, undertook the task of exploring the country to the north of the extreme point occupied by the fur traders." — *Rev. C. G. Nicolay.*

In 1794 this enterprising man ascended to the principal water of the Mackenzie River, which he found to be a small lake situate in a deep Snowy Valley embosomed in woody mountains; he crossed a beaten path leading over a low ridge of land, of 817 paces in length, to another lake, situated in a valley about a quarter of a mile wide, with precipitous rocks on either side, — the head waters of the Frazers' River. On the 19th of July, he arrived where the river discharges itself into a narrow arm of the sea thus showing that a communication between the west and east of North America was open to mankind.

(8) I regret I cannot say when exactly, nor where, his Grace gave his opinion on this subject, and I regret this the more, because I cannot give his Grace's exact words; but of the fact I have no doubt, and I must only trust to your forbearance and memory when I cannot point to the day and place.

(9) "Not long since a very general ignorance prevailed respecting the [Pg 52] Western Coast of North America, and no less general apathy." —*Rev. C. G. Nicolay, 1846.*

(10) "Oh, Squire! if John Bull only knew the value of these colonies, he would be a great man, I tell you, —but he don't." —*Clockmaker, 1838.*

"We ought to be sensible of the patience and good feeling which the people of Canada have shown in the most trying circumstances."-*Mr. Labouchere, Debate on Navigation Laws.*

(11) "Considering all the natural and acquired advantages that we possess for this purpose, it should rather create surprise and regret that our commerce is so small, than engender pride because it is so large."

"We may conclude then that improvements in production and emigration of capital to the more fertile soils and unworked mines of the uninhabited or thinly peopled parts of the globe, do not, as it appears to a superficial view, diminish the gross produce and the demand for labour at home, but, on the contrary, are what we have chiefly to depend on for the increasing both, and are even the necessary conditions of any great or prolonged augmentations of either; nor is it any exaggeration to say, that, within limits, the more capital a country like England expends in these two ways, *the more she will have left.*" —*J. S. Mill, Polit. Econ.*

(12) For "a very large amount of capital belonging to individuals have, of late years, sought profitable investment in other lands. It has been computed, that the United States have, during the last five years, absorbed in this manner more than £25,000,000 of English capital." And how much more, it may be asked, has gone to the continent of Europe and elsewhere?

"When a few years have elapsed without a crisis, and no new and tempting channel for investment has been opened in the meantime, there is always found to have occurred, in these few years, so large an increase of capital seeking investment, as to have lowered considerably the rate of interest, whether indicated by the prices of securities, or by the rate of discount on bills; and this diminution of interest tempts the possessors to incur hazards, in hopes of a more considerable return." — *Mill's Political Economy.*

(13) The Spectator has seriously remarked — "It is sometimes observed, that although taxes have been remitted to the amount of [Pg 53] millions, the revenue has kept up; and that fact is vaunted as the vindication of free trade: but one inference to be drawn from it has escaped notice — it shows that the riches of the country must have increased enormously, and it implies that many of the wealthy are escaping more and more from a due share of the general burden, as taxation is diminished and wealth increased."

"Our exports have increased in value since 1824 from 38 millions to 68 millions."

(14) "It will be found by the Parliamentary Tables, which all can consult, that the amount of money raised in those eighteen years was nearly 1500 millions. The total revenue raised in those years was more than 981 millions; and the total of the money borrowed was more than 470 millions; making, in all, 1451 millions. And it is worth while to note, that, in one of those years, namely, in 1813, the sum of more than 150 millions was raised in revenue and loan, of which nearly 82 millions was loan for the national use; and this in a single year; and that year 1813, in the midst of a dreadful war, and thirty-five years ago; — since when the country has grown much richer."

"Now, dividing the sum of 1451 millions by eighteen years, it appears that 80 millions a year was raised; and, taking the legitimate expenditure of the country, during those eighteen years, at an average of 45 millions a-year, a sum so high as to preclude all cavil, it appears that the country raised and expended eighteen times the difference between 45 and 80 millions, that is 630 millions; notwithstanding which expenditure, let it be observed, the country *got richer and richer* every day." — *Bradshaw's Almanack, 1848.*

(15) "Our economical friends need not be alarmed;—we are not going to propose a large addition to the military force of the empire." — (*Times.*) No:—but before it is reduced and its system interfered with by those who understand not its working, we would strongly recommend the perusal, first of the evidence of Sir Herbert Taylor before the Finance Committee on this subject, and then that of his Grace the Duke of Wellington, and we would ask the intelligent public of Great Britain to reflect well before it allows her present army to be trifled with. We firmly believe our army to be in as high a state of discipline, and as ready "to go any where and do any thing," as it was at the moment his Grace gave up in France the active command of it.

As to our Navy,—let those advocates for reduction go as my friend Captain B——r wished they would,—to the top of the monument, and look around at the forest of masts they will see of vessels coming from and going to all parts of the world; then reflect for a moment on the [Pg 54] power required to defend all their interests; and (if they dare),[see Note 63] then come down and ask for reduction.

We strongly recommend the perusal of the letter of Emeritus on this subject in the *Times* of the 5th February.

(16) "This vast power has penetrated the crust of the earth, and drawn from beneath it boundless treasures of mineral wealth which without its aid would have been rendered inaccessible. It has drawn up in numberless quantity the fuel on which its own life and activity depend." — *Dr. Lardner.*

(17) "It seems a provision of Providence to have formed different races to bring about, by their crossing, an improved state of things. The Teutonic variety is undoubtedly the most vigorous and able, both in body and mind, of all the species of the genus of man that exist, and seems destined to conquer and civilize the world. The Teutonic variety, in its different sub-varieties, agree best with a temperate climate; it is, however, capable of bearing a high degree of cold, but seems to prosper best northward of 45° of northern latitude.

"Teutonic prevailing in Great Britain and part of Ireland, 22,000,000." — *Physical Atlas of Natural Phenomena.* — *Alex. Keith Johnson.*

And it is very curious to observe, that, in the new world, the first colony of Great Britain we reach after crossing the Atlantic is called Nova Scotia; and the last land we should leave after crossing the continent would be New Caledonia; and both in Nova Scotia and New Caledonia (Vancouver's Island) nature seems to have placed great deposits of coal, as if she there intended the industry of man and the advancement of science to overcome all natural barriers between the different nations of the earth.

(18) "A pint of water may be evaporated by two ounces of coal. In its evaporation it swells into 216 gallons of steam, with a mechanical force sufficient to raise a weight of thirty-seven tons a foot high. The steam thus generated has a pressure equal to the common atmospheric air; and by allowing it to expand by virtue of its elasticity, a further mechanical force may be obtained at least equal in amount to the former. A pint of water, therefore, and two ounces of common coal, are thus rendered capable of doing as much work as is equivalent to seventy-four tons raised a foot high."

"The Menai Bridge consists of about 2000 tons of iron, and its height above the level of the sea is 120 feet; its mass might be lifted from the [Pg 55] level of the water to its present position by the combustion of four bushels of coal." — *Dr. Lardner.*

(19) "In addition to the instances of combination between directly competing companies, recent experience has furnished numerous instances of the tendency of smaller lines, sanctioned as independent undertakings, to resign their independence into the hands of more powerful neighbours." — *Report of Board of Trade.* It is not to be doubted, therefore, that all proposed or partly finished Railways in the North American provinces will readily join in the grand undertaking, making one great interest for the whole.

"The traffic of a system of lines, connected with one another, can always be worked more economically and conveniently under one uniform management than by independent Companies. The Company which works the main trunk line, and possesses the principal terminal stations, can run more frequent trains, and make better arrangements for forwarding the traffic of the cross lines, than it could afford to do if two or three separate establishments had to be maintained, and the harmony of arrangements depended upon two or three independent authorities.

"It is found also in practice, that unless a very close unity of interest exists among the different portions of what really constitute one great line of communication, it is scarcely possible to introduce that harmony and accuracy of arrangement which are essential to ensure speed and punctuality. Many important branches of traffic also are apt to be neglected, which can only be properly developed where a long consecutive line of Railway is united in one common interest. Coals and heavy goods, for instance, can be conveyed for long distances with a profit, at rates which would be altogether insufficient to remunerate a Company which had only a run of ten or twenty miles: and thus many of the most important benefits of Railways to the community at large can only be obtained by uniting through-lines in one interest." — *Report of Board of Trade on Railways. Sess. 1845.*

(20) "The two most expensive commodities in England are crime and poverty; of these the most costly is poverty; and the extent of poverty, by its sufferings, vastly increases the amount of crime. You have heard the expenses of poverty. The cost of crime in England and her penal establishments exceeds a million and a half." — *Speech of Francis Scott, Esq. M.P.*

(21) "The circumstance which must first strike any person as extraordinary, in regard to the expatriation of criminals from this country, is the choice of the station to which they have been sent. That a country [Pg 56] which, like England, is possessed of an almost boundless tract of unsettled fertile land within four weeks' sail of her own shores, should, in preference, send her criminals to a territory which cannot be reached in less than as many months, thus multiplying the expense of their conveyance, is a course which requires for its justification some better reasons than have ever yet been brought forward." — *A. R. Porter, Esq., Progress of the Nation.* This system has, we believe, come to a close, and Gibraltar and other places fixed upon; (some in Great Britain); but her convicts ought not to be employed at home if it can be avoided, as they of course

perform the work that would be performed by the labourers of the country, many of whom are thus thrown out of work.

Since the year 1824, a considerable establishment of convicts has been kept up in Bermuda, employed in constructing a breakwater and in perfecting some fortifications at Ireland's Eye. The number at present (1836) so maintained is about 1000.

(22) And why should not English convicts be sent to work in the Rocky Mountains? We all know that the highest peak of Great St. Bernard is 11,005 feet above the level of the sea, and is covered with perpetual snow. Between the two main summits runs one of the principal passages from Switzerland to Italy, *which continues open all winter*. On the most elevated point of this passage is a monastery and hospital, founded in the tenth century by Bernard de Monthon. The French army, under Bonaparte, crossed this mountain with its artillery and baggage in the year 1800; and here Bonaparte caused a monument to be erected to the memory of General Desaix, who fell in the battle of Marengo. If, then, a monastery and hospital have been established since the tenth century, and are still to be found in the old world at such an elevation, and in such a climate, what objection can there be to the establishment of a convict post, under similar circumstances, to open an important road in the new world? We have seen that Sir George Simpson crossed the Rocky Mountains at a height of 8000 feet, but lower passes may yet be found. At all events our soldiers are exposed to every diversity of climate and every hardship; and we see no reason why healthy and powerful criminals should be more cared for. It was also suggested in 1836 — "The gangs might be moved to other and more distant spots, and employed in similar works of utility, and in this way would relieve emigrants from many of the hardships and difficulties which they are now doomed to encounter at the commencement of their settlement." —*A. R. Porter, Esq.*

(23) "It would indeed be a heart-sickening prospect if, in looking forward to the continued progress of our country, in its economical relations, we must also contemplate the still greater multiplication of her [Pg 57] 'criminals'. Still we fear that, for a long time at least, we shall have of them a large proportion, and that arrangements

must be made for their employment. What we have already stated prove that there is no decrease as yet."

One of our periodicals observes—"We have no hope that a class of criminals will ever cease to exist in this country, and it will always therefore be a question, what is to be done with them?.... There are certain conditions directly *essential* to every successful effort for the repression of crime; the legislature should see that the penal code, while as merciful as a reasonable philanthropy can demand, should yet be severe enough to be truly merciful—merciful, that is, to the entire community."

(24) "The flight of a quarter of a million of inhabitants of these islands to distant quarters of the globe, in 1847, was one of the most marvellous events in the annals of human migration. It is nevertheless a fact, that the migration of this year is nearly equal to that of the last." —(*The Times, 1848.*)

"Nor is there any reason to believe that 1849 will witness a diminution in the rate at which this extraordinary process of depletion is going forward; on the contrary, there is every symptom of its probable acceleration." —(*Morning Chronicle, 1849, on Irish Emigration.*)

(25) A few extracts concerning them will be interesting. "The chain of the Rocky Mountains, after being considerably depressed in latitude 46° and 48°, attains a much higher elevation from latitude 48° to 49°, and, continuing in a westerly direction, it separates the affluents of the Saskatchewan and M'Kenkie from those of Columbia or Oregon and other rivers which flow into the Pacific. These mountains appear to decrease again from about 58° to 62° northern latitude, where probably they do not exceed 4000 feet in height; and, still further north, are estimated at less than 2000 feet, between the latitudes of 42° and 58° north. Several peaks rise far above the snow line.

"Wherever the head waters of the rivers, on the east and west sides of the Rocky Mountains, approach nearest each other, there have been found passes through them. Of these, perhaps the most important is the south pass. Between Mount Brown and Mount Hooker, in latitude 52½, another very important pass, offering great facility of communication between the Oregon and Canada, by the waters of the Columbia and the north branches of the Saskatchewan, which, flowing into Lake Winnipeg, gives easy access to Hudson's Bay and the great lakes.

"Among the most awful features of mountain scenery lies the great northern outlet of the territory, resembling the southern in many of its [Pg 58] features, with even more sublimity of character, but especially in having the sources of several great rivers within a very short distance of each other. Here are the head waters of the Athabasca and north tributaries of the Saskatchewan, which falls into Lake Winnipeg; and on the east the northern waters of the Columbia, and the eastern branch of Frazer's River, near a deep cliff in the mountains, which has been called by British traders the Committee's Punch Bowl." — *Rev. C. G. Nicolay.*

The first who penetrated the Rocky Mountains was Sir Alexander Mackenzie, then in the service of the North-West Company. In the year 1793 he crossed them in about latitude 54°, discovered Frazer's River, [A] descended it for about 250 miles, then struck off in a westerly direction, and reached the Pacific in latitude 52° 20'. In 1808 Mr. Frazer, also under the orders of the North-Western Company, crossed the Rocky Mountains and established a trading post on Frazer's River, about latitude 54°; and in 1811 Mr. Thompson, also an agent of that company, discovered the northern head waters of the Columbia, about latitude 52°, and erected some huts on its banks.

[A] Frazer's River has its embouche six miles to the north of the 49th parallel, which defines the United States boundary. It is a mile wide. The country around is low, with a rich alluvial soil.

Fort Langley is twenty miles from its mouth.

Sir George Simpson made a journey of 2000 miles in forty-seven days, from the Red River, viâ Fort Edrington, to Fort Columbia, in 1841; he crossed the Rocky Mountains, at the confluence of two of the sources of Saskatchewan and Columbia, at an elevation of 8000 feet above the level of the sea.

(26) Little, perhaps, did Mr. Pitt suspect the time was to be so near, when that country he had loved so well and served so nobly, would be able to send any quantity of artillery by the mail; and that not eight or ten hours would be required, but hardly three. Would

that he was amongst us now. What could England not hope for, or expect to see realized, in her advanced condition, if directed by such a mind as his.

(27) "It is about 900 miles in length by 600 at its greatest breadth, with a surrounding coast of 3000 miles, between the parallels of 61° and 65° north latitude. The coasts are generally high, rocky, rugged and sometimes precipitous. The bay is navigable for a few months in summer, but for the greater part of the remainder of the year is filled up with fields of ice. The navigation, when open, is extremely dangerous, as it contains many shoals, rocks, sandbanks and islands; even during the summer icebergs are seen in the straits, towards which a ship is drifted by a squall or current, rendering it very hazardous for the most skilful seaman. The transitions of the thermometer are from [Pg 59] 100° to 40° in two days, and the torrents of rain are surprising. Whether in winter or summer the climate is horrible. The range of the thermometer throughout the year is 140 degrees. The sea is entered by Hudson's Strait, which is about 500 miles long, with a varying breadth and with an intricate navigation." — *Montgomery Martin, Esq.*

(28) "The settlement on the Red River, distant from Montreal by the Ottawah River about 1800 miles in lat. 50° north, lon. 97° west, is elevated 800 feet above the level of the sea, contiguous to the border of the Red and Asinibourn Rivers, along which the settlement extends for fifty miles. The soil is comparatively fertile, and the climate salubrious; but summer frosts, generated by undrained marshes, sometimes blast the hopes of the husbandman. The Hudson's Bay Company by the introduction, at a great expense, of rams and other stock, have improved the breed of domestic animals, which are now abundant. Wheat, barley, oats, maize, potatoes and hops thrive; flax and hemp are poor and stinted. The river banks are cultivated for half a mile inland, but the back level country remains in its natural state, and furnishes a coarse hay for the long and severe winter which lasts from November to April, when the Lake Winnipeg is unfrozen and the river navigation commences — viâ Norway house entrepôt — at the north extremity of the lake. The population is in number about 6000, consisting of Europeans, half-breeds and Indians. The two principal churches, the Protestant and Roman Catholic, the gaol, the Hudson's Bay Company's chief build-

ing, the residence of the Roman Catholic bishop, and the houses of some of the retired officers of the fur trade, are built of stone, which has to be brought from a distance; but the houses of the settlers are built of wood. A great abundance of English goods is imported, both by the Hudson's Bay Company and by individuals in the company's ships, to York factory, and disposed of in the colony at moderate prices. There are fifteen wind and three water mills to grind the wheat and prepare the malt for the settlers. The Hudson's Bay Company have long endeavoured, by rewards and arguments, to excite an exportation of tallow, hides, wool, &c. to England, but the bulky nature of the exports, the long and dangerous navigation of the Hudson's Bay, and the habits of the half-bred race, who form the mass of the people and generally prefer chasing the buffalo to agriculture or regular industry, have rendered their efforts ineffectual." —*Montgomery Martin, Esq.*

(29) "It is true there is another communication viâ Montreal, but the country in that direction is not of such a nature as to admit of introducing the rollers or the waggons upon the portages." —*Bishop of Montreal.*

[Pg 60] (30) Mackenzie says, "There is not perhaps a finer country in the world for the residence of uncivilized man, than that which occupies the shore between the Red River and Lake Superior; fish, various fowl and wild rice are in great plenty: the fruits are, strawberries, plums, cherries, gooseberries, &c. &c."

(31) "Of this profitable trade the citizens of the United States possess at present all but a monopoly. Their whaling fleet consists of 675 vessels, most of them 400 tons burden, and amounting in all to 100,000 tons. The majority of them cruise in the Pacific. It requires between 15,000 and 16,000 men to man them. Their value is estimated at 25,000,000 dollars, yielding an annual return of 5,000,000 or 20 per cent. The quantity of oil imported is about 400,000 barrels, of which one-half is sperm. When we add to this profitable occupation for many persons—the value of the domestic produce consumed by them—and the benefit that is thus conferred upon both agricultural and manufacturing interests—the importance of this branch of business will appear greatly enhanced. The whaling fleet of England and her Colonies may be considered as not exceeding at pre-

sent 150; about twenty whales are killed annually in the straits of Juan de Fuca—besides the whale fishery on the banks and coast is important—cod, halibut and herring are found in profusion, and sturgeon near the shore and mouths of the rivers. Already the salmon fishery affords not only a supply for home consumption, but is an article of commerce, being sent to the Sandwich Islands. They are also supplied to the Russian settlements according to contract. The coast swarms with amphibious animals of the seal kind, known by the vulgar names of Sea Lion, Sea Elephant and Sea Cow—but above all with the common seal. The traffic to be derived from these in skins, oil, &c. could not but be lucrative." —*Rev. C. G. Nicolay.*

(32) We are quite aware that the American Lines are made at a much cheaper rate, but we are here advocating a grand permanent link of connexion with Great Britain and all her Colonies and dominions—and however cheaply the Line may be opened, we must not deceive ourselves, but look to a proportional outlay to the greatness of the undertaking. It is in its results and consequences that we look forward to the great benefit and financial return to Great Britain and to her people, both abroad and at home.

(33) It is curious to observe, that in 1822 the Americans themselves fought the battle of England with Russia. The extravagant claims of dominion over the Northern Pacific Ocean and the North-West Coast of [Pg 61] America, which Russia proclaimed at St. Petersburgh on the 9th October,—"It is not permitted to any but Russian subjects to participate in the whale or other fishery, or any branch of industry whatever, in the islands, ports and gulfs, and in general along the coast of the North-Western America, from Behring's Strait to 51° north latitude"—were not passed unheeded by the British Ministry of the day, and it was communicated to the Court of St. Petersburgh that England could not submit to such usurpation. The result of these representations were not imparted to the public; but when these pretensions were made known at Washington by the Russian Minister, the American functionaries protested against them with so much vehemence that it was likely to endanger the amicable relations of Russia and the United States—thus fighting the battle of England as it has since proved. In December, 1823, a treaty was entered into at Washington between Russia, the

United States and England on this subject, and the Russians retired farther north than 55°.

The Marquis of Londonderry was Secretary of State for foreign affairs up to August, 1822, and Mr. Canning succeeded him; and to the watchful care of these two eminent statesmen it may be owing that Russia and the United States did not divide the coast and territory between them.

(34) See Sir Peter Laurie's description of prisons.

(35) In spite of so large a portion of the French population being agricultural, i. e. belonging to that calling in life which developes muscular strength and activity — in spite of that proportion being on the increase as compared with the rest of the inhabitants, it is proved that the number of recruits rejected as unfit for the military service from deficient stature, health and strength, is slowly, surely and constantly on the increase, 40 per cent. are turned back from this cause, and yet the required height is only 5 feet 2 inches.

(36) Several companies have, I believe, been formed for the working of these mines, and the shares, I have heard, were one time rather high. The ore, however, is at present sent chiefly to Boston. The opening of the proposed Line of Railway would no doubt cause a great quantity of it to be sent to Montreal or Quebec and there shipped for England, — enabling the colonies, therefore, to take a greater quantity of our manufactured goods.

Lake Superior. — "Copper abounds in various parts of the country; in particular some large and brilliant specimens have been found in the angle between Lake Superior and Michigan. Henry and others speak of a rock of pure copper, from which he cut off 100 pounds weight." — *Montgomery Martin, Esq.*

[Pg 62] (37) It is true that Montgomery Martin, in 1834, says, "and if Railroads do not take the place of canals, I have no doubt the greater part of Upper Canada will in a few years be intersected with canals. I recommend the latter to the Canadians in preference to Railroads, as by their means the country will be drained, rendered more fertile and *more* healthy."

Since that time several canals have been finished, and I have no doubt, as the country becomes more populous, others may be undertaken for the purposes of drainage and internal communications; but my own personal knowledge has satisfied me that Railroads would be far more useful and a far more ultimate benefit, for there is no doubt that the waters of Canada have a general inclination to subside. Mr. Martin himself says, that "the Lakes Huron, Michigan and Superior, have evidently been at one time considerably higher than they are at the present day;" and although Mr. Martin considers the subsidence of these waters has not been effected by slow drainage, but by repeated destruction of barriers, still the fact shows that the waters are subsiding.

Be this all as it may, I do not think that even Mr. Montgomery Martin himself would suggest a communication by canals from the Atlantic to the Pacific, as well might he recommend a man to travel by a slow heavy coach when a light quick one could be procured; and thus we dismiss the subject of canals.

(38) To encourage this Steam Company, who have so nobly performed their task, Government granted, I believe, £52,000 a year.

(39) Such, for instance, as the carrying letters for a penny, and removing such taxes as bear particularly heavy upon the poor.

(40) The Governor-General, in his opening address to the parliament of the province of Canada on the 18th January, 1849, says— "The officers employed in exploring the country between Quebec and Halifax, with the view of discovering the best line for a Railway to connect these two points, have presented a report which contains much valuable information, and sets forth in a strong light the advantages of the proposed undertaking. I shall lay it before you, together with a dispatch from the Secretary of State for the Colonies, expressive of the interest taken by her Majesty's Government in the execution of this great work."

(41) See Mr. Charles Pearson's Speech on this subject.

(42) The feeling of loyalty becomes so natural to soldiers after a few years service, that it remains impressed upon their hearts in general for the rest of their lives.

[Pg 63] (43) "So great is the fertility of the soil of Canada, that fifty bushels of wheat per acre are frequently produced on a farm where the stumps of the trees, which probably occupy an eighth of the surface, have not been eradicated; some instances of eighty bushels per acre occur; near York (now Toronto) in Upper Canada 100 bushels were obtained from a single acre. In some districts wheat has been raised successively on the same ground for twenty years without manure." — *Montgomery Martin.*

(44) A return of the public money expended in Arctic expeditions was called for. It appears that since the peace, or from the year 1815 to the present, £428,782 have been expended in Arctic expeditions.

(45) Mr. Alderman Sydney said — "that convicts had ceased to be sent to Norfolk Island or New South Wales for a considerable time, and he understood that Lord Grey had been influenced on the question by the perusal of a pamphlet which abounded with information of a most convincing character." — *Times.*

(46) Yes! to the value of its resources we now seem indeed to be awakened. Earl Grey, in his despatch (dated 17th November, 1848,) to Lieutenant-General Sir John Harvey, Lieutenant-Governor of Halifax, says (after speaking of the final Report of Major Robinson on the formation of the Halifax and Quebec Railway) — "I have perused this able document with the interest and attention it so well merits; and I have to convey to you the assurance of Her Majesty's Government that we fully appreciate the importance of the proposed undertaking, and entertain no doubt of the great advantages that would result not only to the provinces interested in the work, but to the empire at large, from the construction of such a Railway." Again, his Lordship speaks of this Railway as "a great national line of communication," and yet on the 4th August, 1848, was issued the following letter from the Treasury Chambers: —

"Sir, — With reference to your letter of the 18th ult. relative to the expenses incurred in the survey of the proposed Line of Railroad between Halifax and Quebec, I am directed by the Lords Commissioners of Her Majesty's Treasury to request that you will move Earl Grey to instruct the several officers in charge of the Governments of Canada, Nova Scotia, and New Brunswick, to cause the proportion of the Railroad survey expenses to be defrayed by each province, to be paid into the commissariat chests on the respective stations.

"I have, &c.
(Signed) C. E. Trevelyan."

"H. Merivale, Esq., &c. &c."

[Pg 64] (47) "We cannot afford to spend £50 a year on a convict at home: let him be sent to a colony where his labour is absolutely necessary, and where, though by his good conduct and his industry he may finally attain a decent subsistence, yet where he will be unable to acquire affluence, and which he will be prevented from leaving for a happier or a richer shore: this will be punishment without sentimentalism, and without vindictiveness." — *The Times*, 19th February, 1849.

"As it is obvious that we must either retain our convicts at home or send them abroad, and the latter can only be accomplished by transportation to a colony, it is obvious (especially after the results of the last experiments) that we must either found a new colony, as in 1783, or adopt the French system, which has nothing certainly to recommend it." — *Globe*, 17th February, 1849.

(48) Lieutenant Synge has observed: "The necessity of protecting works further in the interior against hostile tribes of Indians is a formidable impediment to their successful prosecution at present." How easily would this impediment be removed by paying these Indians with guns, blankets, &c., and employing them to guard the convicts and the works.

(49) "The hostility of the Indians overcome, (or what for the present would more effectually restrain England's advance, the possibility of their sufferings being increased by the progress of civilization,) the passage of the Rocky Mountains may rather prove a stimulant, as it will be the last remaining obstacle, and, attention being called to the subject, may urge to exertion the talents of such men as have elsewhere conquered every natural difficulty, however formidable." — *Lieutenant Synge, "Canada in 1848."*

(50) "More especially the very great opportunities afforded by the cessation of convict labour in our Australian colonies should not be overlooked. The great present pressure in these colonies, in consequence of the want of such labour, should be removed in connection with the relief and profitable employment of portions of our surplus home population." — *Same Author.*

(51) "To derive from these measures the chiefest benefits they may confer, the work must be executed under the superintendence of the Imperial Government." — *Same Author.*

[Pg 65] (52) "Great as is our civilization and intelligence, compared with the empires of former days, we have no right to think that the goal of prosperity and glory is attained. England has by no means reached the zenith of earthly power; science is as yet but in its infancy; the human mind has scarcely arrived at adolescence; and, for aught we imperfect beings know, this little island may be destined by Divine Providence to continue as a light unto the heathen — as a nucleus for the final civilization of man." *Preface to "Taxation of the British Empire," published in 1833.*

(53) This of course would only be a temporary arrangement previous to their being sent to distant parts.

(54) "So long however as the empire's heart is overburdened by a surplus multitude, it should be remembered that most fertile and lovely tracts of country, many times larger than England, exist in the body of that empire, which never yet within the knowledge of man have yielded their fruits to his service. A manifold-multiplied value also is given to every part of the connected communication between it and the Atlantic, and thereby also to every part of British America, when once the goal of the Pacific is attained." — *Lieut. Synge.*

(55) An officer whose character stands high both in the navy and in the army — whose talents have long been exercised in the North American Colonies — who is acquainted with their value, and who well understands their naval and military defences.

The writer of this letter sailed from Cork on board H. M. frigate Pique, in January, 1838, with a wing of the 93rd Highlanders, under the command of Lieutenant-Colonel Macgregor, and he is happy in having this opportunity of publicly thanking Captain Boxer, the officers and crew of the Pique, for the great kindness received by every individual of the regiment. And he cannot do otherwise than refer particularly to the officers of the gun-room, who must have been exceedingly inconvenienced by having a large party of officers joined to their mess, and who yet had the tact and politeness to show they never felt it. It was a long and stormy passage of six weeks from Cork to Halifax, but it was a happy and a merry one; although a damp was at first thrown over us by the sudden death from accident of a serjeant of the Light Company, and another poor fellow was washed away from the chains during the passage.

[Pg 66] (56) "We have now enjoyed more than thirty years peace, and when it was proposed to invest the Capital, which we could so readily throw away on arms and gunpowder, upon actually productive works, the cry was raised of impending ruin and bankruptcy. The lodging of deposits with the Accountant-General was to result in 'ruinous, universal and desperate confusion.' The money was lodged, and no ruinous confusion took place. The Acts were obtained, and ruin was again predicted; 'where was all the money to come from?' The money has been got, £112,100,639 has been raised in the course of three years, involving, it is true, much suffering to some classes, but not to the nation at large." — S. *Smiles on Railway Property.*

(57) If once it was understood by the public that Government had taken the initiative, and was determined to assist and see carried out a great national work such as has been suggested, there is no doubt that many people who are now paying high poor rates would join together, and a variety of small Emigration Companies would be formed to assist poor people to emigrate, and these poor people would willingly and cheerfully quit their native land, when they had before them the certain prospect of immediate employment; and if the penny postage was added to the system, they would be nearer to England in the North American Colonies, than the poor people of England and Scotland were to each other only a few years back.

(58) "Four hundred millions of people yet to be introduced into communication with the rest of mankind! What a prospect for the merchant, the manufacturer and ship owner. But there is still a higher and holier prospect. Four hundred millions of active and intelligent human beings have to be brought within the pale of Christianity! Wary stepping, too, it will require to enable us to succeed in realizing either of these objects. To assist us, an abler man for the task could not be found than the author of the work before

us." — *Liverpool Standard, Review on Montgomery Martin's recent Work on China.*

(59) "Nobody can doubt that the western coast of North America is about to become the theatre of vast commercial and political transactions, and it is impossible to estimate adequately the value which may soon accrue to every harbour, coal mine, forest and plain in that quarter of the globe." — *Morning Chronicle, 15th Feb. 1849.*

(60) On which Line the mails could travel from Halifax to Frazer's River in six days, and the electric telegraph connect these oceans — space vanishing under that magic power.

[Pg 67] (61) See Montgomery Martin's second edition on Railways, Past, Present and Prospective.

(62) There is not an individual of the 93rd Highlanders, so long quartered in the highly flourishing city of Toronto, who would not, I feel well assured, join me in every grateful feeling to its inhabitants, and every wish for their happiness and welfare.

A great number of the men of the 93rd have settled at and in the neighbourhood of Toronto.

(63) "The British 'supremacy of the ocean,' which has been a boast and a benefit, has become a necessity. If I were Prime Minister of England, now that the Corn Laws are repealed, I should not be able to sleep if I thought that the war marine of England was not stronger than all the nations combined, which there is the least chance of ever being engaged in a conspiracy for our destruction." — *Edward Gibbon Wakefield.*

(64) "Canada, which receives the greater number of emigrants, we are by all accounts only peopling and enriching for the Americans to possess ere long." — *Art of Colonization, Edward Gibbon Wakefield.*

I trust that the British North American Colonies will, in reply to the above remark, send forth such a voice of attachment to their mother country that will encourage her people at home and embolden them to come forward in aid of great colonial measures, resulting as they must do in universal benefit to the empire.

In page 100 of the work just above quoted we read—"The Banker's argument satisfied me; but he was not aware of a peculiarity of colonies, as distinguished from dependencies in general, which furnishes another reason for wishing that they should belong to the empire—I mean the attachment of the colonies to their mother country.... I have often been unable to help smiling at the exhibition of it. In what it originates I cannot say."

I cannot but deeply regret the use of these expressions, coming as they do from the pen of so influential an author. Has be forgotten or does he not feel that

> "Cœlum non animum mutant qui
> trans mare currunt?"

And surely from those who left their native land, carrying with them the literature of the day and the remembrance of her glory, it was not likely that there should spring up a generation otherwise than strongly attached to

> "*That* fortress built by Nature for her-
> self,
> Against infection and the hand of
> War?"

[Pg 68] Well, indeed, has Lieutenant Synge remarked, "Let it also be remembered by those who would argue the defection of Canada, or other British provinces, from the history of the past, what were the circumstances attending the last revolt (and only one) of British Colonies."

"Let the regret with which those colonies revolted be also borne in mind! Generations have succeeded, yet in the hearts of many of the best and noblest that lingering regret remains; not that the revolt took place, not that it was successful, but that it was rendered necessary." I shall only add, I agree most perfectly with the author on the Art of colonization when he says, "But whatever may be its cause, I have no doubt that the love of England is the ruling sentiment of English Colonies."

(65) "The Americans would have readily agreed with us upon this boundary question, when it was of no practical moment."— *Edward Gibbon Wakefield.*

This assertion requires proof.

(66) My friend Lieutenant-Colonel Pottinger has brought to my notice, that the time of transit from London to the west coast of Ireland will be nearly as follow, vis.

| To Holyhead | 8 | hours |
| Holyhead to Dublin | 4 | " |
| Dublin to the west coast of Ireland | 4 | " |
| | — | |
| In all | 16 | |

It may therefore be worthy of consideration whether there could be established at one of her ports on the western coast, so often spoken of as the nearest point of embarkation for British America, an Emigration Company, which would greatly benefit Ireland by causing a large traffic through the centre of that country.

(67) Dr. Hind, in speaking of the convict Colony of New South Wales, says—"If then the question be, what can be done for this Colony? Begin, I said, by breaking up the system—begin by removing all the unemancipated convicts. I do not undertake to point out the best mode of disposing of them; but let them be brought home and disposed of in any way rather than remain. There is no chance for the Colony until this preliminary step be taken. But these measures, if carried into effect at all, must be taken in hand soon. Time—no distant time, perhaps, may place this 'foul disnatured' progeny of ours out of our power for good or for harm."